DOMINIQUE SIEGLER-LATHROP

The Secrets of Needlepoint

TECHNIQUE & STITCHES

DOWN EAST BOOKS
Camden, Maine

Copyright © 1997 by Buchet/Chastel • Pierre Zech Éditeur, Paris.
English text translation © 2000 by Dominique Siegler-Lathrop.

Photography by Gaston Bergeret
Cover design, U.S. ed, by Faith Hague
Computer graphics by Deb Clark, Prop Art
Drawings by Armor Le Bihan
Layout: Francine Kergosien

Printed in China

2   4   5   3   1

Down East Books / P.O. Box 679, Camden, ME 04843
Book orders: 1-800-766-1670

LIBRARY OF CONGRESS CATALOGING-IN-PUBLICATION DATA

Siegler-Lathrop, Dominique, 1939–
    [Secrets de la tapisserie à l'aiguille. English.]
    The secrets of needlepoint: technique and
stitches / by Dominique Siegler-Lathrop.
        p.   cm.
    Includes bibliographical references and index.
    ISBN 0-89272-504-4
    1. Canvas embroidery.   I. Title.
TT778.C3 S533 2000
746.44'2—dc21
                                        00-029516

Equipment and Preparation

Technique

CONTENTS

PREFACE

Having dabbled in all kinds of needlework for many years, I finally ended up with a needlepoint business about ten years ago. I didn't know too much about needlepoint then, but as I got further into it, I discovered a completely new art form. Indeed, I realized that needlepoint is not simply a piece of painted canvas on which one pulls a needleful of wool through millions and millions of individual holes in a repeated stitch.

To me, a canvas represents a painting in wool. It has to be treated as a painting, using many different colors of wool to create hues and shades, sometimes mixing two colors together in the same needleful. Or it can be a canvas that demands different stitches to make it more interesting. Or again, it can be a design requiring a particularly attentive approach to a background, with perhaps a different stitch or a distinctive color. One thing is certain: a canvas demands thoughtful planning, imagination, and a good measure of love.

These varied aspects of needlepoint dealing wholly with artistic matters also have to be gathered into a disciplined technique, able to render wool embroidery on canvas into beauty and form.

I learned some rudiments of the technique of needlepointing in Paris. As my business developed, so did the technique, which I taught to as many people as I could. I dealt with a lot of needlepointers, and discovered that until they came to my shop, none of them had ever heard of a discipline peculiar to needlepoint. People usually just moved from counted cross-stitch embroidery on linen or cotton to embroidery on canvas, using the same method and the same stitch—a big mistake, as the two are radically different.

In the meantime, I did some research in French and English books dealing with needlepoint and could find nothing describing the kind of method I was using and teaching. The technique yields such good results that I was anxious that everyone should know about it, and this is the reason behind *The Secrets of Needlepoint.* If you follow exactly the instructions outlined in this book, you will become a professional very quickly.

The book is making headway in France as people realize there is more to needlepoint than they had thought. It has become a useful tool in our classes here in the shop in Paris, and I hope very much you will discover the *art* of needlepoint through it.

Bonne chance!

Dominique Siegler-Lathrop

Tapisseries de la Bûcherie
2 rue du Haut Pavé
75005 Paris FRANCE

Telephone: 33 1 40 46 87 69

URL: www.bucherie.com
e-mail: needlepoint@bucherie.com

VISITING www.bucherie.com

My website is a "going on forever" kind of project, not only because of the infinite technical aspects (which, as everyone who has established a website knows, are perfectly horrendous), but also because maneuvering hundreds of photographs of needlepoint designs onto the site is a challenge of some magnitude. I must here pause in grateful thanks to two of my boys, who have done all the work: Felix Rust established the original site, and Marc Rust is currently updating it and adding his technological expertise. Surely, without them, I would not be where I am today.

The site contains a great number of French needlepoint designs — from small canvases (sold as kits, with wool hand-dyed in Aubusson, one of the tapestry capitals of France) to large wall hangings, chair coverings, etc. The collection is typically French, illustrating all the styles from the medieval *mille-fleurs* tapestries, such as the famous unicorn hangings in the Metropolitan Museum in New York and the Cluny museum in Paris, to the contemporary style of today. It comprises hundreds of models for armchairs of the sixteenth through nineteenth centuries. More pictures and information on the art of needlepoint and its history are being added all the time, as well as descriptions of French furniture of different periods.

FOREWORD

Whether you are an expert or a beginner, here is a remarkable manual that shows clearly and simply from A to Z all you need to know about needlepoint. Dominique Siegler-Lathrop is an expert and a passionate advocate of the art of needlepoint. She has dug, dissected, and analyzed all that the art of needlepoint comprises, and this book is the fruit of this search for perfection.

Being myself just as interested in whatever has to do with canvas and with tapestry in general, I opened my workshop in 1970. Many adepts who went through the Atelier Mozet, are still calling me, though I am now retired. Since the time I've known Dominique, our mutual passion has brought us close together and has caused us to share many ideas and discoveries.

Through the years I evolved a technique that enables one to needlepoint any design with a minimum amount of gestures and a minimum amount of time. I am very lazy by nature, and the necessity of having to constantly change colors of wool exasperated me. The thought occurred to me to use as many needles as there were colors of wool and to work somewhat like weavers do. From these first steps, this technique was then perfected by Dominique.

In this book you will find everything: how to thread a canvas needle, how to work different stitches, how to interpret a design. One chapter I particularly like—"Technique, the Servant of Art"—opens the door to many different possible interpretations. The drawings are superb, concise, and easily understandable. The numbered and colored diagrams of the stitches are original and allow for a more rapid understanding of the various possibilities the needle offers for the interpretation of a graphic design.

This book is the indispensable manual, the Bible for all canvas advocates. It was needed on our library shelves.

Marie-Thérèse Mozet, 1996

THE SECRETS OF NEEDLEPOINT

During the Middle Ages and the Renaissance, wonderful fancy-work was stitched on hemp cloth with much

imagination, taste, delicacy, and excellence of execution. Wool and silk, gold and silver thread were used. However, no manual or other records have come down to us concerning the method of stitching on canvas used in those distant days. About two centuries ago, "penelope," or double-thread canvas, was invented. This gave rise to another kind of stitchery: the *tramé*. First, a picture is drawn on the canvas. Then wool threads are attached horizontally across the double weft to mark the colors. Wool of matching colors is then used to stitch over the horizontal *tramés*. (See stitch #43, p. 80.)

The counted stitch was also invented as a means to avoid having to paint the canvas. This entails stitching on a blank canvas by following a design on graph paper, each square representing a stitch. Counted stitch commonly meant half-cross or cross-stitch. These two methods of working—*tramé* and counted—became very popular, and everyone began to work in these two ways. Once the designs were finished, the background was done in half-cross or basketweave.

Today, the art of stitching on canvas has more or less been lost. After all, *tramé* and counted stitch are purely technical means of reproducing a design, as they permit no personal interpretation. However, these methods are today just as good and they are still quite popular. The counted stitch, especially, is a lot of fun to execute.

However it is possible now, thanks to acrylic indelible paints—which are easy to use and quick-drying—to work on painted or printed canvas. This progress allows us to work freely, without limitations as to color or kind of stitch.

Needlepoint requires no long apprenticeship, and if you follow the instructions carefully, you will master the art in a very brief time. Let us first talk about equipment and preparation.

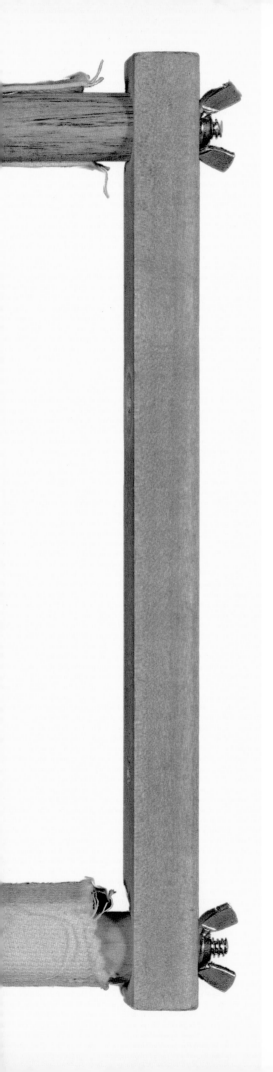

Equipment & Preparation

---◆---

The Frame

How to Fix the Canvas to the Frame

A tapestry frame should be rectangular or square, never round (this would damage and deform the canvas). A heavy cloth tape is stapled onto the crossbars of the frame, and the top and bottom edges of the canvas are then sewn to the tape of each crossbar. Before starting, use an indelible felt pen to mark the exact center of each tape as well as the center of the canvas edges. Place the canvas, design face-up, on a table, then put the crossbar, tape-side down, on the canvas, matching the pen marks (see illustration below).

Sew the tape from the crossbar of your frame onto your canvas.

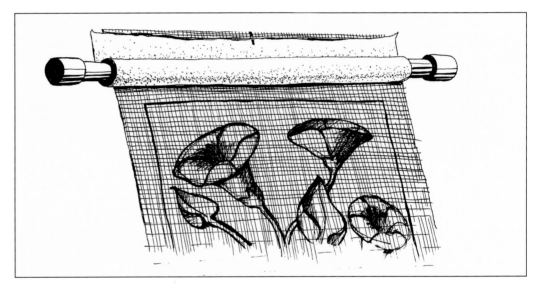

Sew the one edge of the canvas to the tape with heavy-duty thread, roughly but solidly. Repeat this procedure with the other edge. (You can also attach the tape with a sewing machine, but that is not required; the thick thread does the job perfectly.)

Fit the crossbars of the frame into the side bars and turn them until the canvas is taut. You will begin to stitch at the top, so any extra canvas should be rolled around the bottom crossbar. As your work progresses, you will roll the canvas onto the top bar and it will unroll from the bottom one.

How to Position the Frame

There are varying widths of frames available, to accommodate whatever size of work you undertake. A small frame can be placed on a table corner and held in place with a weight, such as a brick or a metal weight. A wider frame can be put across sawhorses, or the arms of a chair, or on cushions. Some frames come with supports that clamp onto a tabletop. All frames must be positioned in such a way as to leave space underneath.

There are also floor frames, which are more costly, but more beautiful, more stable,

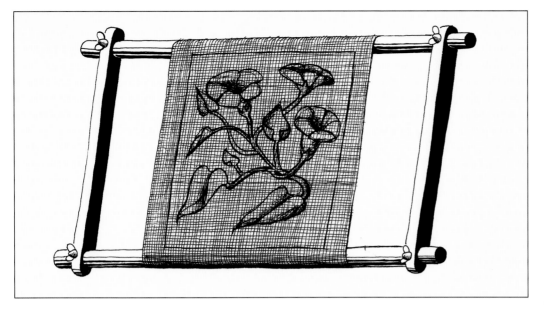

Position your frame so that you are comfortable and both your hands are free.

and easier to handle. The only disadvantage is that a floor frame takes up room, for it is a piece of furniture in its own right, whereas a hand frame can be put in a closet or carried in a bag. The choice is up to you, but it is imperative that you do use a frame of some type.

Why Use a Frame?

Without a frame, it is not possible to stitch correctly. With the canvas held securely by the frame, both of your hands are free to stitch. When you follow the instructions in the "Technique" chapter, you will find that both hands must be used—one on top of the canvas, one underneath.

Needlepoint canvas is starched and stiffened, and would quickly become limp if held with the hands. It would lose its shape and the stitches thereby would lose their uniformity. Canvas held on a frame does not lose its stiffness, and its weave stays in place. The more tightly the canvas is stretched on the frame, the easier it is to pass the wool through the holes. Canvas should be stretched tight as a drum.

Moreover, a tapestry worked on a correctly stretched canvas will undergo a minimum of deformation—or none.

Finally, a hand-held canvas inevitably will begin to unravel on the sides, as the weave is very loose and fragile. Canvas is the support for the stitches that are going to adorn it. Canvas and wool form *together* a very solid surface, but separately, neither material has much identity. While waiting for the magical meeting between the two, canvas and wool, let us take great care of both, starting with the canvas, which cannot be stitched unless taut and stiff.

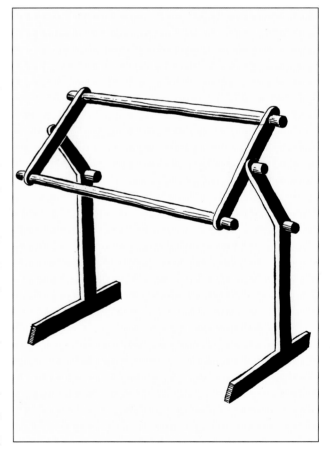

In order to stitch correctly, it is essential to stretch your canvas on a frame.

Types of Canvas

There are two types of canvas: monofil, or unifil, and penelope, or double-thread canvas. Generally, monofil canvas is adequate for slanted or diagonal stitches, whereas penelope canvas is perfect for straight stitches.

Both penelope and monofil canvas come in dozens of mesh sizes. They can range from the very smallest mesh for fine embroidery to big mesh for rugs, while fabric lengths can go from 20 inches to 60 inches (50 to 150 centimeters).

Color is generally white or beige, but the very fine-gauge canvas is manufactured in several other colors as well.

Needles

Tapestry needles have either a rounded or a pointed end, and a large eye to pull wool through. They come in different sizes, depending on canvas mesh.

How to Thread a Tapestry Needle

Wrap the wool around the top of the needle and remove the needle, leaving the folded wool end held tightly between your thumb and index finger. *Without loosening your hold on the wool,* push the eye of the needle between thumb and index finger, into the wool. Your needle is threaded. Never wet the wool or crush it between the teeth as you might do for cotton thread. Once your needle is threaded, you have a needleful.

With a little practice, you will be able to thread your needle without looking.

The Knot

You might be tempted to just hold the wool underneath the canvas and not make a knot at all. Actually, it is easier and faster to use a knot; you will cut it later (see p. 18).

How to Make a Knot

First, thread your needle, then hold it with the eye end between your right thumb and index finger. With your left hand, take the tail of the wool and bring it over the needle toward you, and hold the end with the thumb of the right hand.

With the left hand wrap the wool around the needle two or three times and place your right thumb and index finger over the wrapped wool. Slide this mass along the needle, over the eye, and all along the wool thread to the end. Your knot is done—you'll never miss it once.

 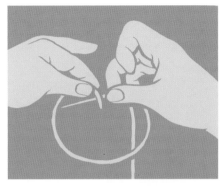 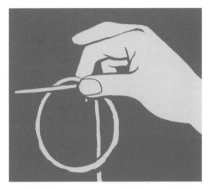

You cannot miss a knot if you do it this way. You can even teach it to your children.

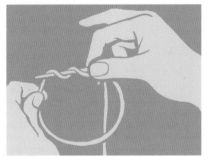 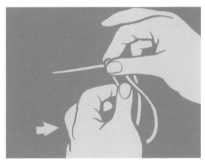 

The Wool

It is preferable to use a fine wool, which makes it possible to combine colors in the same needleful. More important, by adding or subtracting wool strands, you can vary the thickness of stitches on the same canvas. For example, you can stitch on the same canvas a cross stitch using four or five strands, and a quarter stitch using just one or two strands. A fine wool yarn, then, allows great diversity in color and stitches.

Scissors

Small curved scissors, or thread-cutters—a kind of flat scissor with beveled blades—are the most practical type to use for needlepoint. The scissors are held flat against the canvas when used, to avoid the danger of cutting the canvas itself.

Thread-cutter

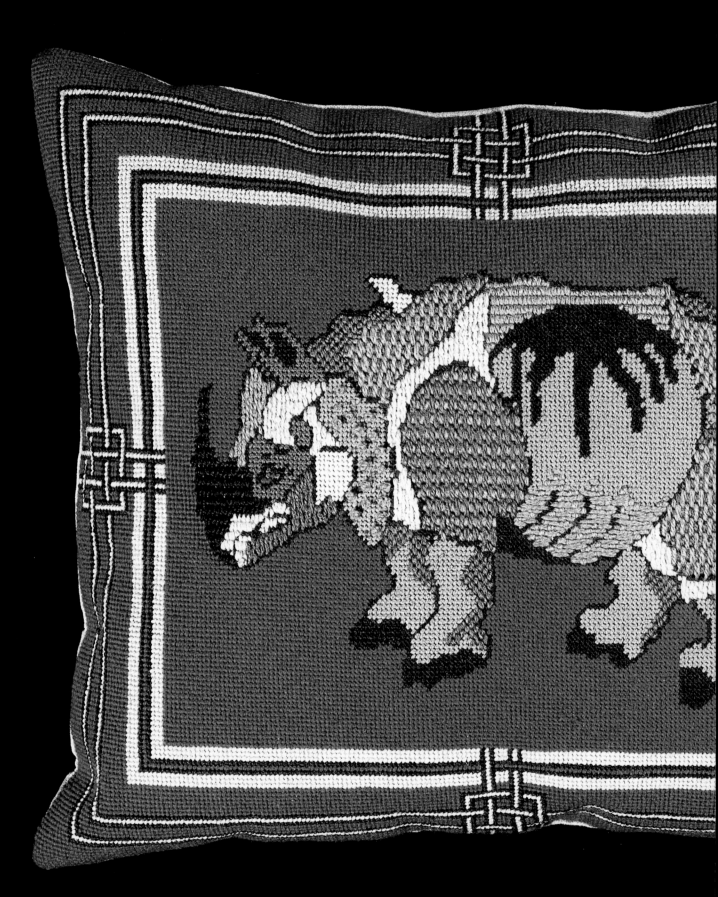

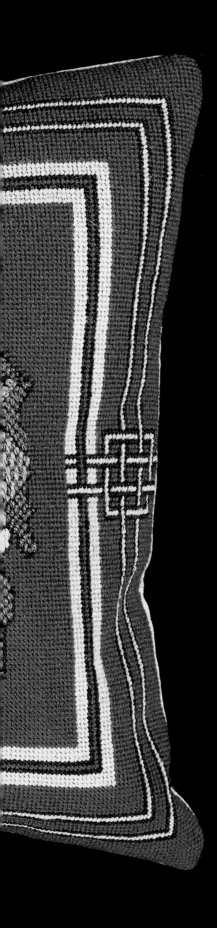

Technique

The Technique of Needlepoint

How to Begin and End a Needleful

You are comfortably seated in front of your canvas, which is stretched onto the two crossbars of your hand or floor frame. You should have within your reach:

- a pincushion with several dozen tapestry needles
- your various colors of wool
- scissors or thread-cutter
- a thimble (very useful for pushing the needle)

Thread your needle (using a length of about 30 inches, or 75 cm) and make a knot.

Push the needle from the right to the wrong side, so that the knot is *on top* of the canvas, one to one and a half inches (2 or 3 cm) from your first stitch.

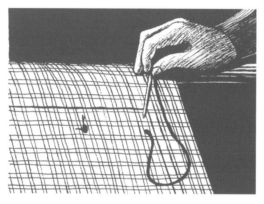 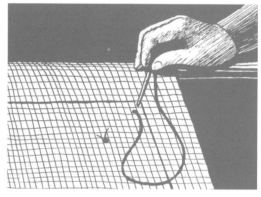

• When doing a straight stitch, the knot will be in the row, in direction you are stitching.

• If you are doing a diagonal stitch, the knot will be toward the bottom, diagonally.

As you work, the wool tail underneath will be covered, and you will cut the knot when you have stitched up to it.

In the same way, when you reach the end of a needleful or need to change colors, pull the needle through from wrong to right side one to one and a half inches (2 to 4 cm) from the last stitch, as you did to begin the needleful, but in reverse. Remove the needle and leave the tail as it is—you will cut it when you have stitched close enough to it that it is in your way. You do not need to make a knot.

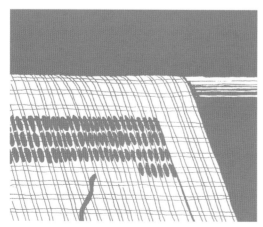 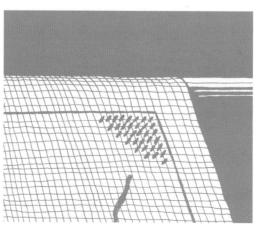

How to Cut the Wool

Once you have reached a knot or the end of a needleful, pull the wool and cut it as close as possible to the canvas, so that the end bounces back underneath, leaving no trace whatever on the surface.

To avoid cutting the needleful you are actually working with, leave it under the canvas when you are about to cut a knot or a tail. This will clear the area. Bring the needleful back up right away to continue stitching.

If, inadvertently, you cut the wrong strand, you must undo enough stitches to salvage a sufficient length (about three inches) to terminate the wool as described above. Then thread another needle and catch up the stitches before continuing your work.

What Do You Do with Your Hands?

You use both hands throughout the process. Even if you have never done this before, you will get used to it quite quickly. Once the habit of working with both hands is established, you will work at a rather fast pace. The hand on top pushes the needle down through the canvas; the other hand pulls the needle and pushes it back up. It does not matter which hand does what.

The hand on top also makes sure that the wool is always straight, not twisted. Underneath, the other hand guides the thread and makes sure there are no knots or irregularities. Both hands are always occupied, and always held close to the canvas.

When you push the needle from right side to wrong side, place your little finger in the loop in order to keep the thread from twisting as the needle is pulled underneath. Push the needle all the way to the eye with your thimble, if you are wearing one. The other hand will pull it more easily, and, if needed, will give a little extra push on the canvas to disengage the eye more rapidly. In the same way, it is very useful to give a little push on the top of the canvas with a finger to free the eye, as it can sometimes be difficult. These little motions help prevent the wool from pulling on the canvas, which needs to stay as taut as possible. This also protects the wool, which must always stay beautiful and full.

Take Good Care of the Wool

In the final analysis, the only visible result of your needlework is the wool surface. All the rest—the support, the beautiful hand painted design—will have disappeared.

Almost all the techniques described in this book have as a goal to protect the wool and render it to its best advantage. Any yarn, even if it is of the best quality, can be reduced to a pulp if it is mistreated. Your movements must be rapid but never forceful. Never pull hard—slide the wool instead, put it gently in its rightful place. Never push a needle through a finished stitch; insert it *next to* the other stitch (in the same hole). If you have to undo more than a dozen stitches, that length of wool will be worn out. Do not use it again. Terminate it (push it out as you do for the end of a needleful), and start a new needleful. If you love the wool, it will love you back.

Most of us unconsciously turn the needle in our fingers as we stitch, so that the wool twists and loses its lightness and its volume. It is necessary therefore to untwist the wool constantly. You can let the needleful hang by itself underneath the canvas and it will right itself by turning. You can also turn the needle between your fingers (above the canvas) to undo the additional twisting. With practice, the second way is the best because you do not waste time and you can learn to constantly twist the needle slightly in the right direction so that the thread is always straight.

To review: Both hands work simultaneously, one on top, one beneath the canvas. They both stay close to the canvas, guiding and checking the wool. In order to pass the needle's eye through the canvas smoothly and to avoid pulling hard (thus damaging the canvas or the wool, not to mention your hands), give a little push on the eye against the canvas with a finger. You should never be tired, and you should be able to acquire some speed. You never need to look under the canvas, except to admire your work—which will without a doubt be impeccable!

Where to Start?
Work in Rows, with Multiple Needles

The technique of needlepoint used here is radically different from any other method you might have heard about. You are going to work *in rows*—horizontal, vertical, or diagonal, depending on the stitch and the canvas. You will work everything all at once—that is, the background and the design—stitch by stitch, row after row, so that, when you roll up your canvas as the work progresses, the rolled-up part will be completely finished. This way of working produces the most beautiful results—canvases that are perfectly worked, without mistakes or forgotten stitches, smooth and well balanced.

Let us start at the top right-hand corner. If you are working a straight stitch on penelope canvas, you will place your knot toward the left, as shown in the first illustration on p. 18. If you have a monofil canvas and are doing a slanted stitch, place the knot as indicated in the second (right-hand) illustration on p. 18 and pull up the needle in the top right-hand corner. You will proceed to stitch, one hole after another, along the row (horizontal, vertical or slanted). Whatever the angle of the row, the method is the same.

Moving from One Color to the Next

You will continue to work until you arrive at the place where you have to change color—either at the beginning of a design, if you were doing background, or a change of color in the design. Push the needle you are working with up into the hole in the next row that has that color. Leave your needleful on the right side of the canvas. (After you pull the wool through to the right side, just drop the needle; it saves time.)

Never leave a needleful on the reverse side of the canvas while you are working. The thread would get in the way and get caught up in the other stitches. This would be a mess and would require all the stitches to be taken out in order to free the wool thread.

Continue your row. Take a new needleful in the new color, make a knot as usual and place it as before, a little further on, and you will continue to work in the row, stitch after stitch, without ever skipping a hole.

Right side

Wrong side

When you get to a new color, you start the same procedure by adding a third needleful, and you continue, adding as many needlefuls as needed. At the end of the row, start the next row directly underneath, this time going in the opposite direction. All the needlefuls have been correctly placed from the previous row. You take them up as they present themselves, you stitch, push the needle back up in the next row down, drop your needle, pick up the next one, and so on.

Picking Up the Same Color Farther On

Do not jump from one area to another of the same color if there is a separation of more than an inch. If the space is too wide, terminate your needleful, and start another one when you get to the new place.

Ending a Needleful

When you end a needleful, do not shorten the tail by cutting it. You will cut it later, after the wool underneath has been covered up by subsequent stitches. No matter how long the tail end is, do not cut it. For example, you might be at the end of a needleful and have only a very short segment left, or you might have a long thread of a color no longer needed. Either way, wait until you have covered the wool underneath before cutting a strand (close to the canvas). In this way, you do not waste wool, and if you have made a mistake, you can always retrieve the wool. Always save the wool.

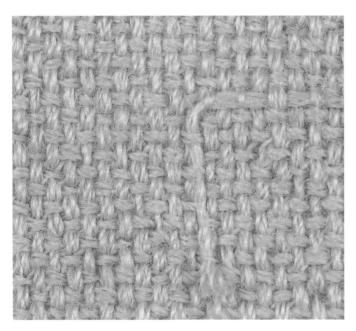

Do Not Tack Ends on Reverse Side!

Never (but never!) tack the end of a needleful into stitches on the reverse side of your work. There is not enough room. Forcing the tail end inside existing stitches destroys the harmonious look of the work and compresses the canvas out of shape.

Only the last piece of wool, the one that terminates the canvas, must be tacked—but watch out! You cannot bury the needle into the stitches, reaching down to the canvas. Rather, you must pass the needle near the surface of the stitches and make several right angles to secure the tail (see photo at left).

Direction of Stitching

Always work a stitch from the bottom upward; that is, you begin each stitch in a vacant hole and go into an occupied hole in the preceding row. Go from an unstitched row below to a stitched row above.

How to Undo a Stitch

If the needle is on the wrong side of the canvas, you must bring the wool back up: unthread the needle, and, very delicately, take up the stitch with your needle and pull up the wool gently. Then re-thread your needle.

If the needle is on the right side, pull the thread toward the stitched part of the canvas in order to create a space in the hole. Carefully put the needle through the space and pull it out underneath, making very sure not to snag the wool.

Note that you never have to turn the canvas to the wrong side, even when you are undoing a stitch.

Avoid Pushing the Needle up through a Stitched Hole

If possible, do not push the needle up from the wrong side through a stitched hole or you will damage the wool, for the needle cannot avoid snagging the stitch already in place. Nevertheless, there are certain stitches (the crossed basketweave, for example) where this is unavoidable. In that case, try to push the needle up *next to* the wool already stitched, in the corner of the hole, never in the middle.

Did You Forget a Stitch?

If you have forgotten a stitch and you are too far away to go back, take one single wool strand and a small tapestry needle. Turn the canvas over, and, very delicately, tack the thread on the surface an inch or two away (just as you do when ending the last needleful—see the p. 22 photo). Turn the canvas back and do your stitch as many times over as there are strands of wool. For example, if your needleful normally consists of four strands, you go over the stitch four times with one strand. Then you terminate your needleful as shown on p. 22. Generally, if you are attentive, you should never miss a stitch. The technique of working in rows keeps you from making this kind of mistake.

Thread Tension

Do not pull the wool too tight. Remember that you are pulling on the thread twice—once with each hand, up and down. Place your thread so that it is neither too tight nor too loose. A good way of seeing if you are stitching correctly is by holding your frame against the light. If you see light through the stitched canvas, your stitches are too tight, or the wool is not thick enough for the mesh size. If stitched too tightly, canvas will shrink, and you can lose several inches of surface. And, to be honest, it isn't very handsome. A correctly stitched canvas is full without being loose, and just tight enough to be thick. Needlepoint should always have a look of opulence, of warmth and abundance.

How to Pull the Needle

When you are stitching, do not pull the wool toward yourself as you would if you were embroidering on linen or sewing. Pull the thread directly upward when you are above the canvas. In the same way, pull the thread directly downward when you are pulling from underneath. This keeps the canvas from becoming distorted.

Conclusion

There are several advantages to the row-by-row method of working. Aside from its simplicity and the short period of apprenticeship needed to learn it, the result is that of

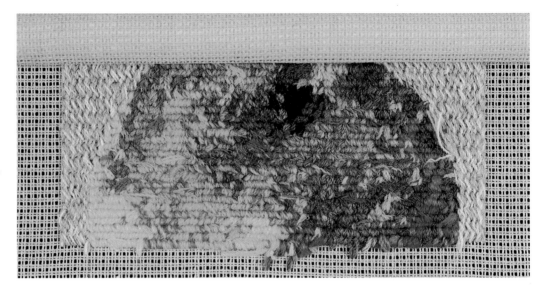

Reverse side of
Apple. *Painting on*
penelope canvas by
Nadine Oosterhof.
Partly stitched,
Gobelin and brick.

a professional. Everything appears at once as you progress, which is more satisfying than having to go back to fill up empty spaces. And it is practically impossible to make a mistake—for example, skipping a stitch. Finally, the work is impeccable, on the right side as well as on the wrong side, where not a loose strand can be seen. This method of stitching also gives a much more solid and longer lasting piece of work. This is because, as you are working stitches next to each other, the wool underneath passes into part of the previous stitch. All the stitches adhere to each other, thus forming a uniform matrix. Furthermore, the tail ends from all the needlefuls help reinforce the solidity of the work since they are anchored and completely hidden.

Lastly, the fine execution of needlepoint provides the satisfaction of an art form that can give marvelous results and is within anyone's reach.

Reverse side of a rug
(style Napoleon III).
Counted stitch,
crossed basketweave.

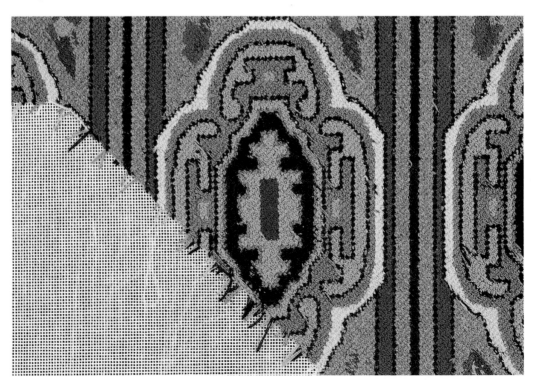

Technique, the Servant of Art

Solid-Color Designs

The technique described in the preceding pages is indispensable for counted stitch on canvas as well as all designs in solid color. A solid-color design does not have gradations of hues; that is, it does not have different color hues within a given design element. Each design component is a single, even color.

For this kind of work, you do not have to worry about adding a personal interpretation to the design. You stitch exactly according to the colors using the row-by-row method just described, working stitch after stitch and changing color whenever required.

Solid-color Louis XIII style design by Tapisserie de France, cushion stitched by Mme Paulette Bertin, Gobelin on penelope canvas.

Designs with Graduated Hues

Now let us see what you will do if you have chosen a design with hues that melt into each other in subtle gradations. You will study your design, think about the colors of wool

Mille-fleurs created and stitched in Gobelin and brick by Nadine Oosterhof. An example of graduated hues.

you have in hand, choosing perhaps to mix two colors in one needleful—in short, you are going to interpret your design, add your own personality. This needlepoint canvas will really be yours—a unique piece.

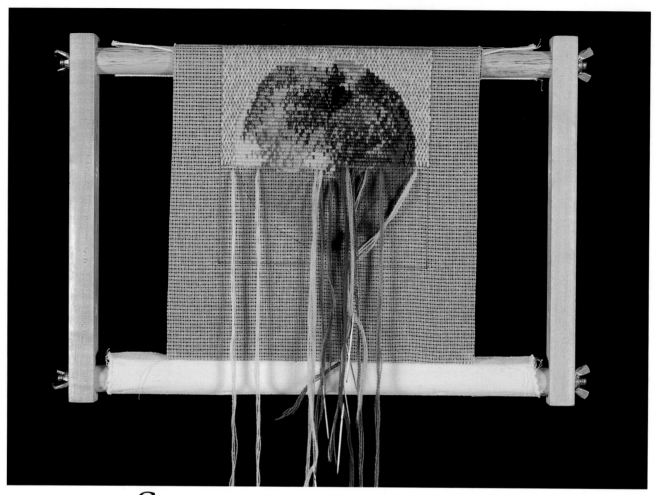

Apple. *Created and partly stitched by Nadine Oosterhof. An example of a "divergence." Note how the needlefuls not in use are left hanging in front of the work.*

Small Divergences Are Allowed . . .

While using this technique, you will take a few liberties so that you can interpret your ideas on the canvas. As you are progressing with the work, you may want to finish a flower petal while you are inspired, or do a few stitches to define a shadow, etc. By all means, do it, but then go back immediately to the row, which you will continue to stitch as usual. In other words, what is important is that the tapestry be really beautiful. Technique is the support of artistic interpretation. If from time to time you feel led to spill over, just return as soon as possible to the row in progress. Be careful, however: if you take too many liberties and start stitching independent large areas, you'll have difficulty placing your knots and terminating needlefuls. Just as when you work counted stitch or a solid-color design, when you roll the canvas on the top crossbar, everything that is rolled up must be completely finished. It is necessary to work row by row most of the time and to break out of the row only for a few stitches at a time, not for a complete motif.

Another Exception to the Rule

We are concerned here with compound stitches. In order to complete a compound stitch, it might be necessary to work different simple stitches in several directions and over more than one mesh. These compositions thus necessitate working by area rather than just one row at a time. Nevertheless, the basic rule is to advance the whole work at once, even though it may be impossible to work by row.

Take a Step Back for Perspective

When you work, be attentive to the whole design. You will work in detail while thinking of the whole. Be careful with the outlines of a motif. Be generous; give priority to the design. The background should not overpower the design.

Rhinoceros. Design by Toni McPheeters, stitched by the author. Example of a work done "by area."

Directoire *cushion.
Tapisseries de la
Bûcherie. Horizontal
Gobelin and brick
on penelope canvas.
Border is double
straight cross.*

Shells. *Designed by
Nadine Oosterhof.
Basketweave on
monofil. Note the
sewn-on braid
trim enhancing
the needlepoint.*

Backgrounds

The background is just as important as the motif. An error in background can ruin or detract from a beautiful design. On the other hand, a well-thought-out background can turn an otherwise unremarkable design into something special.

Background Colors

There are several ways of determining the color of a background. The color is chosen to enhance the design. It can be neutral, or, on the contrary, very bright.

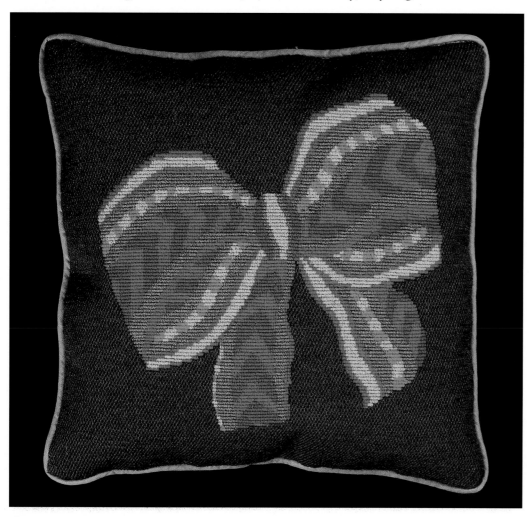

Design by Tapisserie de France, stitched by Mme Nelly Vildé. An example of a strongly colored background that makes a coherent ensemble with the ribbon. Gobelin and brick stitch on penelope.

Stitches and Motifs for Backgrounds

Background stitches can be different from the stitches used for the design. A different stitch, even in the same color as the motif, or neutral, creates sufficient contrast. A background can also be a design. On the *Directoire* cushion (top of page 30), note the lozenge background worked in two different colors. Woven fabrics can also make interesting backgrounds; small canvases were sewn into fabric as an inlay to make the *Shells* cushions shown on page 30.

Design by Tapisserie de France. Needle-pointed by Mme Nelly Vildé. Two small squares inlaid into an oblong cushion.

Borders

A border gives a "finished" aspect to needlepoint. There are a great variety of stitches that can be used for borders. The small Louis XVI pillow shown below has three rows of bourdon stitch over different counts of mesh. Note also the border on the *Directoire* cushion, p. 30, in double straight cross stitch.

Floral Louis XVI design by Tapisserie de France. Cushion stitched by Denise and Isabelle Monnier.

Materials

Aside from the background and design, the choice of materials plays an important part in making a tapestry unique. Besides choosing colors and stitches, you must also

Fruits. *Designs by Tapisserie de France. Centers stitched in wool and silk, basketweave on monofil. Wide border in wool, fancy stitch. Needle-pointed by Marie-José Chauvin-Berthillon.*

think about which materials to use. Normally, a tapestry is stitched with wool. As indicated previously, a fine wool has much more diversified uses than a thick wool.

It is also interesting to use silk, or satin finish cotton thread, or linen thread, or finally, silver and gold thread. Silk and linen brighten the texture of wool and can be used for either background or design. Be careful, though: silk, cotton, linen have a much shorter life than wool. Consequently, it is a good idea to use these materials in limited amounts and to mix them with the more durable wool whenever possible.

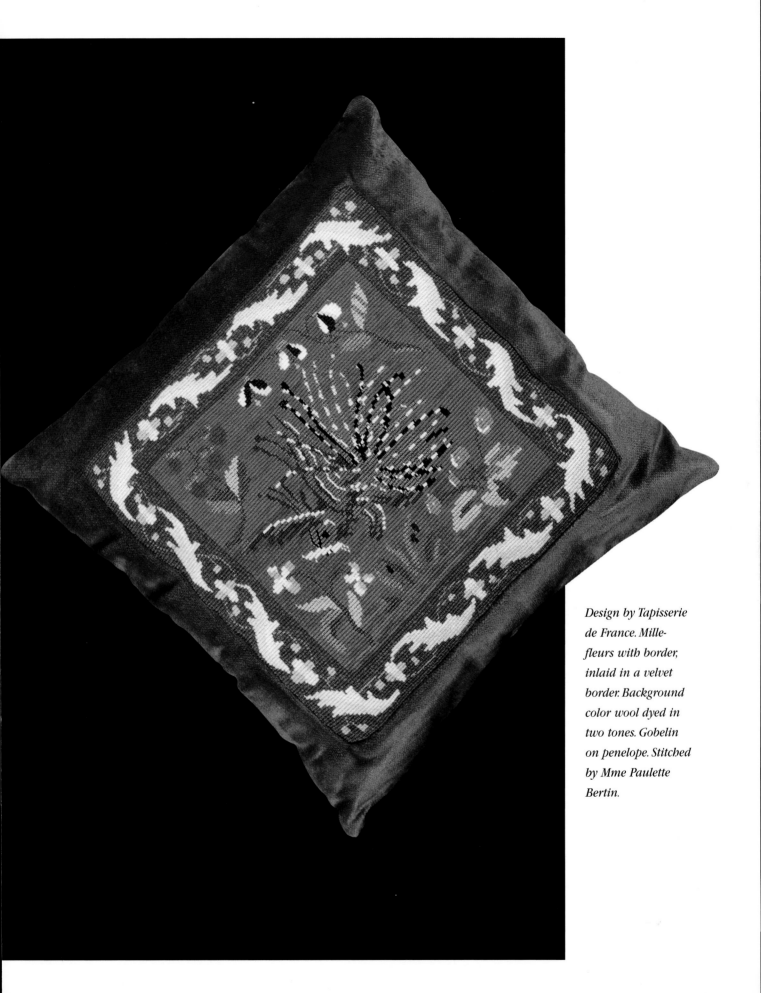

Design by Tapisserie de France. Mille-fleurs with border, inlaid in a velvet border. Background color wool dyed in two tones. Gobelin on penelope. Stitched by Mme Paulette Bertin.

More Explanations and Advice

Mesh Counts

A mesh is the thread that runs across the canvas horizontally. We say that a stitch is worked over one mesh if the wool covers one canvas thread: it comes out from the hole underneath the mesh and goes in the hole above it. Certain stitches are worked over several meshes. On monofil, or unifil, canvas, a mesh is a single canvas thread. On penelope canvas the threads are paired. With penelope, then, one mesh implies *two* threads.

Anchor Stitches

When you make stitches that are longer than three meshes, in order to attach the wool to the canvas, make a small "anchor stitch" over one mesh (for penelope) or a basketweave stitch (for monofil [p. 42]) before starting the long stitches, and do another one at the end of the needleful. These small stitches fix the thread on the canvas, which will not be otherwise well anchored by the long stitches. They will disappear from sight under the long stitches. The goal, obviously, is to make sure the needleful is held down at both ends.

The Rule of the Two Canvas Threads

A stitch should always cover two canvas threads, on the reverse side as well as the right side. The two threads can be in the form of a cross, one above the other, or next to each other. In other words, you must go over two canvas threads in any direction. Because of the very loose weave of the canvas, if you cover only one thread, your wool will tend to shift and leave a gap when it is pulled. On the other hand, if there is already a stitch in place, it is possible to work a strand over a single canvas thread since the canvas is already held by the first stitch (as, for example, in the crossed basketweave stitch, p. 48). In that case, there is no risk of the wool moving about. Normally, you should *never* work a stitch over a single canvas thread, on either the right side or the wrong side.

Be careful! Penelope canvas, which has two threads per mesh, *can* be worked over only one mesh. Monofil, with only one thread per mesh, *cannot* be worked over one mesh. In order to work a straight stitch on monofil, you must work over two meshes.

Wool Thickness

For stitches reaching farther than three meshes, you must add one or more wool strands to your needle to make a thicker thread that will cover better. For small and tight stitches, a lesser thickness is appropriate. Naturally, this depends upon the density of the canvas.

Canvas holes should stay in their original places. If, while you are working, the canvas threads begin to push against each other, your wool is too thick and takes up too much room. On the other hand, if the wool is too thin, the canvas will show through and your tapestry will have a skeletal appearance. Remember that needlepoint should always be thick and give an opulent aspect.

The Importance of Stitch Thickness on Reverse of Canvas

In needlepoint, the wool density on the reverse side is just as important as it is on the right side. Don't try to economize wool by not covering the reverse side of the canvas. Never be stingy—it shows immediately.

To explain the problem more clearly, here is an example using the bourdon stitch. The drawings below show the correct way to work this stitch.

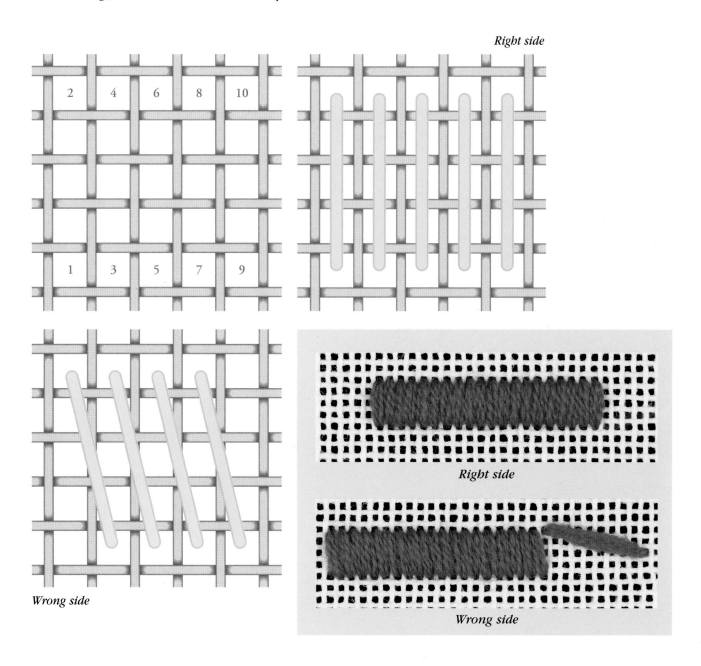

Right side

Wrong side

Right side

Wrong side

Note the double thickness of wool, covering both sides of the canvas. On the wrong side, both the anchor stitch and the wool end have been covered by the long stitches. The double thickness also gives a rounded aspect to the stitches, which is very pretty.

Now look at what happens when we try to economize on wool. There is only one thickness on the right side and nothing on the other side.

Wrong method of stitching. The canvas is not covered on the reverse side and the stitches look too thin on the right side.

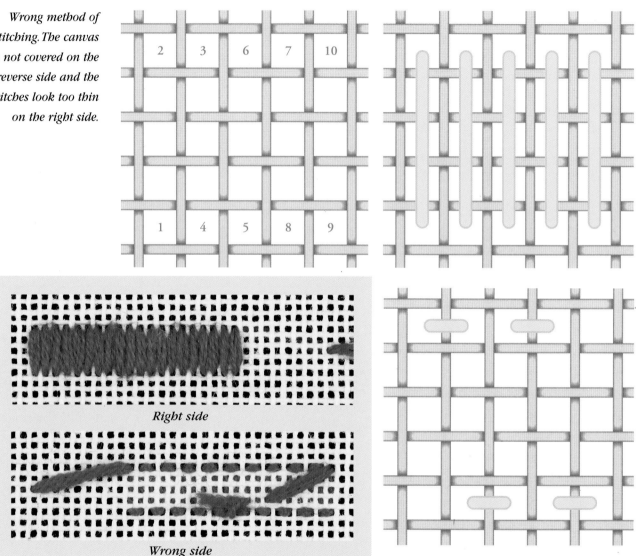

Right side

Wrong side

On the wrong side, the anchor stitch, which is not covered up, is all that holds the wool thread, the knot above having been cut, leaving the wool end flapping. Furthermore, the rule of never stitching over only one mesh has not been observed. Thirdly, the aspect of the stitch is meager, and the canvas shows through in some places.

Working Long Diagonal Rows

Your canvas, being rolled on a frame, presents a limited rectangular or square surface, which can pose a problem when you do basketweave and other stitches that are worked in diagonal rows. You do not have to waste time unrolling and rerolling your canvas at the end of every row. Instead, you should simply stop when you can't go any further.

If you are stitching a large surface in a single color—a background perhaps—stop your rows in a zigzag pattern, as shown in the drawing at right. Stopping on a straight horizontal line will leave a visible transition.

On the other hand, if you are using lots of colors, you can stop on a straight line. The photo below shows a rug with no single-color area, so each section of the work was stopped on a straight line. Note the top left corner, where the rows were stopped previously, and the bottom right, which is the stop line for the segment currently being worked.

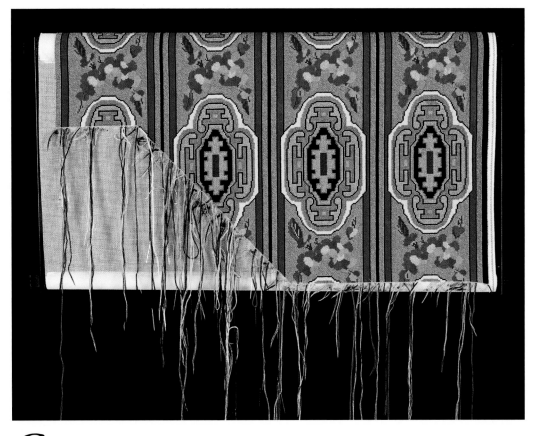

Napoleon III rug, counted, crossed basketweave, stitched for Claudine Cros by the author. Example of stopping work on a straight line.

Canvas Color

Canvas color can be important. For example, do not use a white canvas when you are going to be working with black wool. Natural or beige color is neutral and is a good background for all colors.

Choosing the Right Stitches

When you are starting a project, think about the stitches carefully, whether simple or compound. Certain stitches are not appropriate for surfaces that will be often touched or handled (chair seats, armchairs, stools). Also, stitches made on larger mesh canvas will not be as durable as stitches worked on finer-meshed canvas. Very long stitches are more apt to be torn or caught. So the choice of stitches must be planned according to function. For seats, stools, and rugs, don't even think about using fancy stitches.

Wool Thickness in Relation to Mesh Gauge

As explained above, canvas comes in different mesh gauges (number of meshes per inch), consequently, the holes are different sizes according to the canvas. You must figure out the wool thickness in relation to canvas mesh gauge and in relation to the stitch you have chosen. It is important to work with fine wool so that you can control the thickness of your working thread by adjusting the number of strands in each needleful.

Watch for Dark Ends under Light Wool

When you begin or terminate a needleful of very dark wool, be sure that the dark color won't show if you are stitching with light-colored wool over it. In most cases you won't have any problems, but be vigilant. If you think the dark will show through, begin and end your needleful in another direction. If that is not possible, you must do as you would for the last needleful (see p. 22, "Do Not Tack Ends on Reverse Side!").

Making a Gradual Color Transition

There are two reasons for working a slow color change—that is, a change so slow that it is almost unnoticeable. The first reason is a planned change: you have a surface with a design or background that gradually changes hues. The second reason is that you are going to run out of wool and the new wool is a different hue (different dye lot or different manufacturer). In either case, you follow the same procedure.

If you are using four strands, begin by threading your needle with one strand of the new color and three of the old. Later you will change to two new plus two old, then three new and one old, and finally, four of the new. Work as much surface with each combination as you deem necessary. Be alert; if you wait until the last minute to notice you have no more wool, you may not be able to make these gradual color changes.

In order to remember the color gradations step by step:

(starting with 4 strands) 4+0 ; 3+1 ; 2+2 ; 1+3 ; 0+4.

Monofil or Penelope?

Stitches on Monofil

Generally speaking, one can work all the stitches on either type of canvas. But monofil mesh, being composed of single rather thick threads, will often show between straight stitches unless the wool is very thick. However, monofil canvas is very good for diagonal stitches, which tend to cover it completely since the holes are square and close together.

On monofil

Stitches on Penelope

On the other hand, penelope—which is woven with double threads—gives a different aspect to tapestry. The holes are farther apart and more elongated in height. The mesh threads are thinner than for monofil, and do not show between straight stitches. Straight stitches, then, are more suited to this type of canvas.

In order to show the difference in aspect for the two types of canvas, we have worked the same stitch over the same number of mesh on both monofil and penelope. The stitch is a bargello. Note the elegance of the stitch on penelope. In contrast, on monofil these stitches have a flattened look, and the wool threads are not as tight, showing the canvas in certain places.

Nonetheless, there are many straight stitches that are more handsome or more practical on monofil and many slanted stitches that are better on penelope. So there is no absolute rule concerning straight or slanted stitches, but, whenever possible, penelope is preferable for straight stitches, monofil for slanted stitches.

In the following pages, the stitches are explained in a way that is practical and easy to understand. After trying all the stitches on both types of canvas, we have chosen what we thought worked the best. Nevertheless, you can try another type of canvas than the one indicated on the drawings, or you can try another way of stitching.

On penelope

Generally, all of these stitches can be done on both types of canvas, on the condition that you work penelope as monofil (see petit point, p. 43) for those stitches which are indicated only for monofil. However, in such cases, it might be simpler to instead use a very fine-meshed monofil rather than to go through the trouble of separating all the penelope threads.

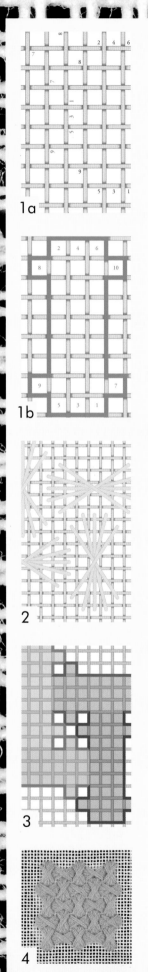

1a

1b

2

3

4

How to Read the Stitch Instructions

For each stitch you will find the following details:

1. A penelope or monofil grid, with numbers (a).

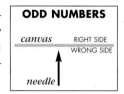

Odd numbers indicate that needle is pushed from wrong side of canvas to right side.

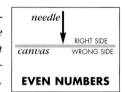

Even numbers indicate that needle is pushed from right side of canvas to wrong side.

By following the numbers with your needle, you will do the stitch.

When several stitches form a figure—called a compound stitch—a blue outline is traced around the numbers (b), forming a figure that is then shown on grid #3.

2. Grid showing the stitch formed by following the numbers in grid #1.

3. When needed, a grid representing the compound stitches in relation to each other. The blue figure is the first to be stitched, red is the second, green the third, and mauve the fourth. Always refer back to grid #1 to work the stitch.

4. Photo of a worked square, to give an idea of what the stitch really looks like.

5. Written instructions indicating whether the stitch covers the canvas entirely or partly, and specifying the required thread weight: fine, medium, or thick. This section also includes any special instructions.

Colors of the Diagrams

Blue   The first row for simple stitches;
             the first figure of the first row for compound stitches.

Red   The second row for simple stitches;
             the second figure of the first row for compound stitches.

Green   The third row for simple stitches;
             the first figure of the second row for compound stitches.

Mauve   The fourth row for simple stitches;
             the second figure of the second row for compound stitches.

The Needlepoint Stitches

THE BASIC STITCHES

There are only four small, tight stitches in needlepoint. All the others (several hundred) are compound stitches derived from these four basic stitches. Stitches have come down to us through embroidery or through ancient motifs in Byzantine art, for example. The more tight and small the stitches, the more solid the tapestry. Consequently, for armchairs, chairs, stools, it is preferable to use these stitches and reserve the more imaginative stitches for cushions, wall panels, and the myriad other articles that can be made in needlepoint.

Basketweave

1

Not to be confused with the continental stitch, which is worked on penelope in horizontal rows, the basketweave stitch is worked on monofil canvas in diagonal rows.

The basketweave stitch can also be called *petit point* when it is worked on very fine monofil canvas (or penelope, by separating all the threads), or *gros point* for much larger-meshed canvas, and finally, quickpoint for very large rug-size stitching. In any case, it's always the same stitch.

It is necessary to understand the composition of the canvas when working this stitch, which constitutes the basis for all needlepoint made to cover chairs, armchairs, and stools. The canvas is composed of horizontal and vertical threads. A stitch should always cover two canvas threads. Each stitch will cover a vertical and a horizontal thread where they intersect.

Working Up or Down a Row: How to Decide

You will work across your canvas in alternating diagonal rows. When you are working a row where the vertical threads of your canvas cross over the horizontal ones, you proceed *down* the row. On a row where the horizontals cross over the verticals, you go *up* the row. The stitch is always worked the

Petit point, gros point.

same; what needs to be understood is the direction of the row.

Another way of looking at it is that the horizontal thread must be covered while going up the row, like climbing the steps of a stair-case. The vertical thread must be covered while going down the row; they are like the posts holding up the banister on which you lean while descending the stairs. Are you going up or down?

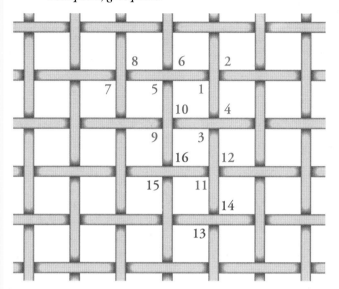

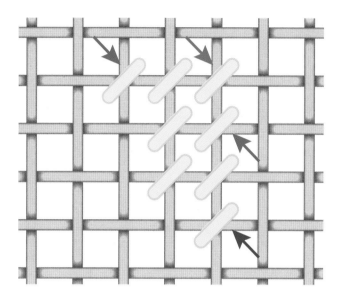

Petit Point

When you've really learned basketweave and your row directions, you'll be able to do *petit point* on penelope. You use the needle to separate the double canvas threads so that they look like monofil, and work the stitches exactly as described above. The horizontal and vertical canvas threads are always your guides to do *petit point* impeccably. A photo of the wrong side of basketweave can be seen on page 21.

Center: petit point. Border: bourdon stitch (see p. 115).

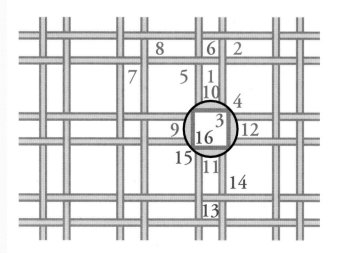

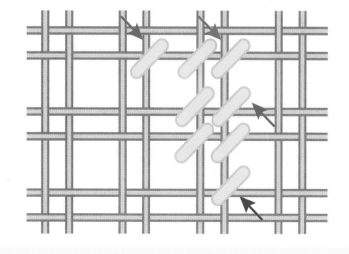

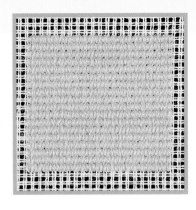

Gobelin Stitch

This is a straight stitch done on penelope canvas. It creates a texture uncannily similar to that of handwoven tapestries. Gobelin stitch can be used for chair coverings, but it is especially good for wall panels because a straight stitch is always more elegant than a slanted one for that particular purpose.

The Gobelin stitch is executed in horizontal rows and fills every horizontal space, so that there is only one vertical thread between stitches. The double horizontal mesh stays intact. Remember that in needlepoint you must always cover at least two canvas threads with each stitch. Stitch length can vary with Gobelin. Here it is worked over one mesh.

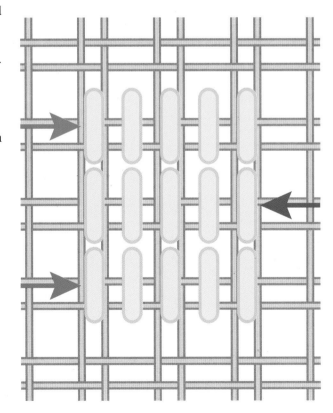

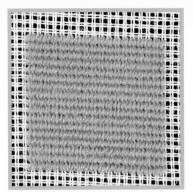

Horizontal Aubusson

This stitch should be worked on penelope. (It can also be done on monofil but is not as handsome.) It is slightly inclined but is worked in horizontal rows.

Instead of inserting the needle directly above the hole where it just emerged, as for Gobelin stitch, you put it in the space immediately to the right of the vertical canvas thread, separating the double mesh.

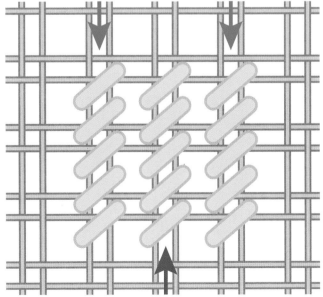

Vertical Aubusson

Still on penelope canvas, this stitch is worked in vertical rows. It is slightly inclined, as in the horizontal Aubusson, and gives the impression of corduroy.

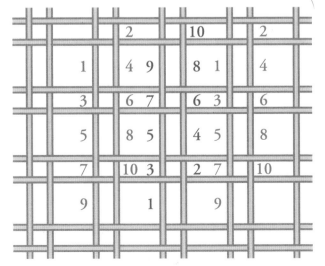

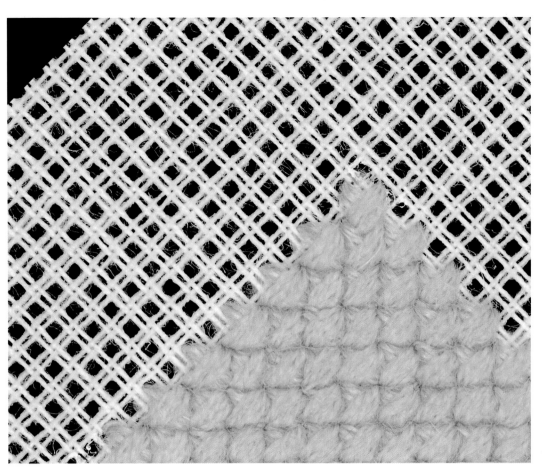

THE CROSS STITCHES

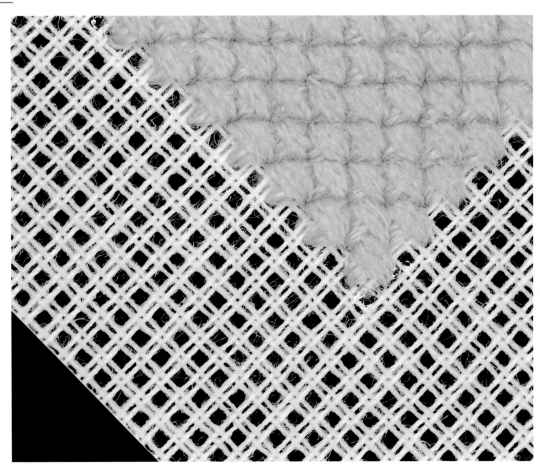

Crossed Basketweave

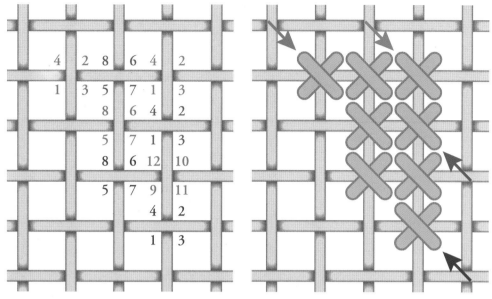

This stitch can be worked only on monofil. It is basketweave (explained on page 42) but with a second stitch added, forming a cross. It is worked exactly like basketweave, in diagonal rows. This stitch is perfect for rugs, for it is very thick and strong, also hard and tight, forming an ex-

tremely solid and rigid surface. Do not try to work this on penelope canvas, for it will

not have the same effect; you won't get the thickness and durability necessary for a rug.

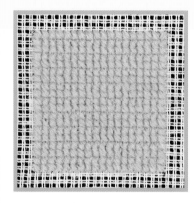

Cross Stitch

Worked on penelope canvas in horizontal rows. You can do each cross one at a time (diagram A) or work a half cross along the row, then go back along the row to stitch the other half of the cross (diagram B).

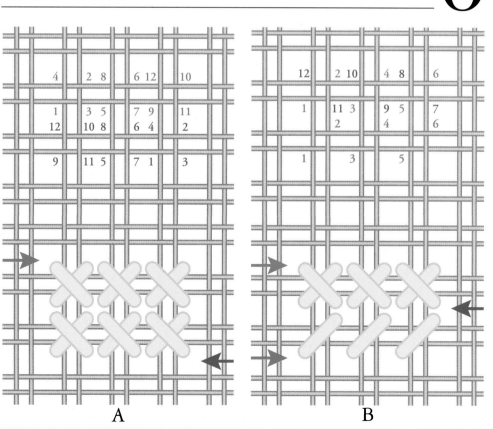

A   B

Underlined Cross

This stitch is very full, giving an impression of richness. Work on monofil. Medium wool thickness.

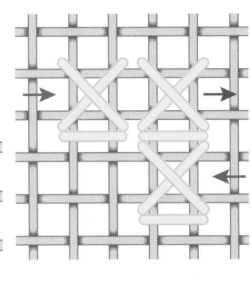

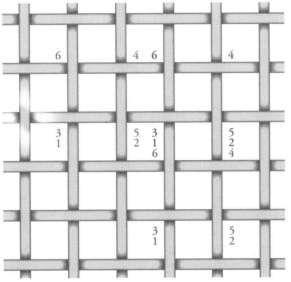

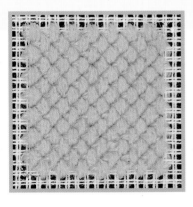

Upright Cross

Worked in horizontal rows. A very easy stitch to do, and very handsome. The second row is offset from the first row. Use it for a background. Medium wool thickness. Covers the canvas very well.

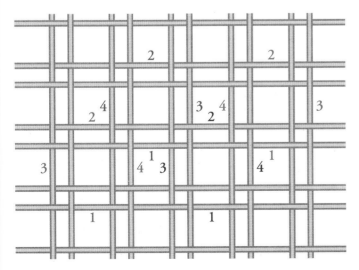

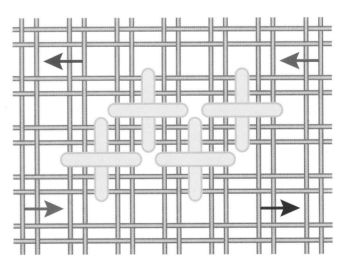

Italian Cross

Worked on monofil in horizontal rows. Medium wool thickness. Does not entirely cover the canvas.

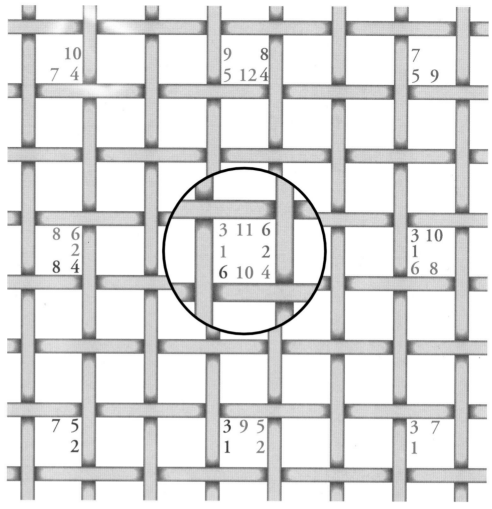

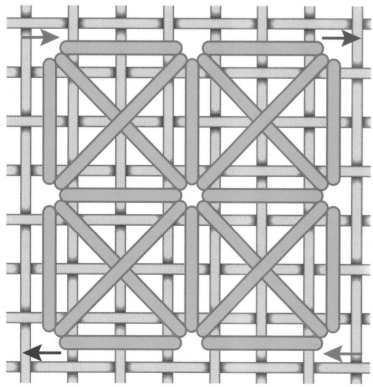

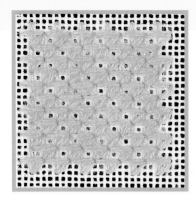

Diagonal Cross

Can be stitched on monofil or penelope in diagonal rows. Use a thick wool thread. Does not entirely cover canvas.

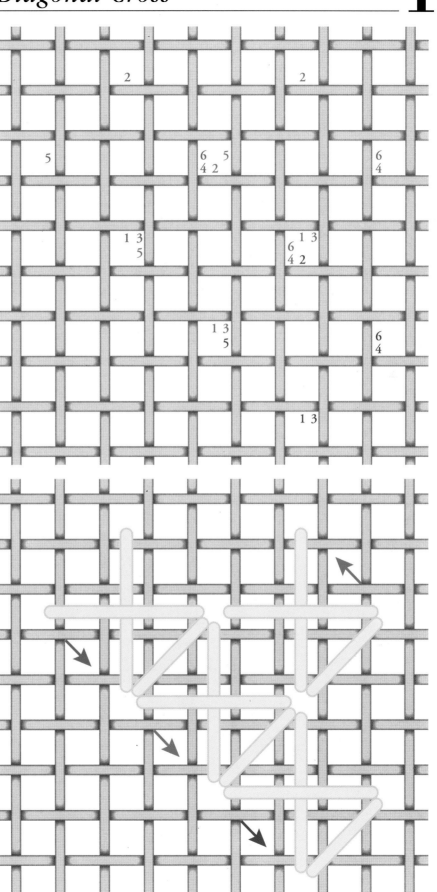

Double Straight Cross

11

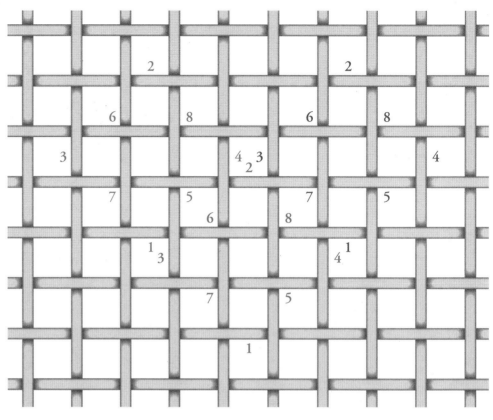

Worked on monofil in horizontal rows. (Can be worked on penelope by separating all the canvas threads as for *petit point*.) Medium wool thickness. Covers canvas well. Very lovely stitch for borders (see border of *Directoire* cushion, p. 30).

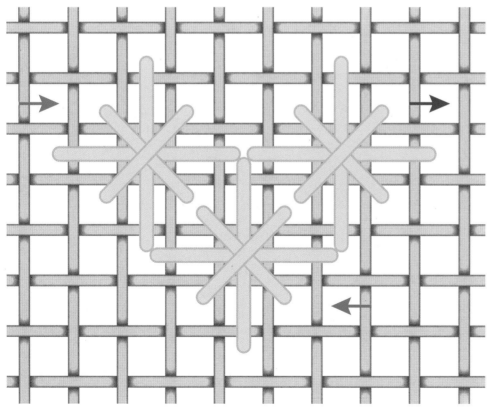

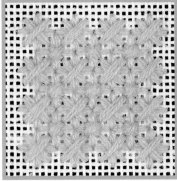

Moss Stitch

Worked on monofil in horizontal rows. The second row offsets the first row, the stitch of the second row being slightly different from that of the first row. Use a thick wool. Does not completely cover the canvas.

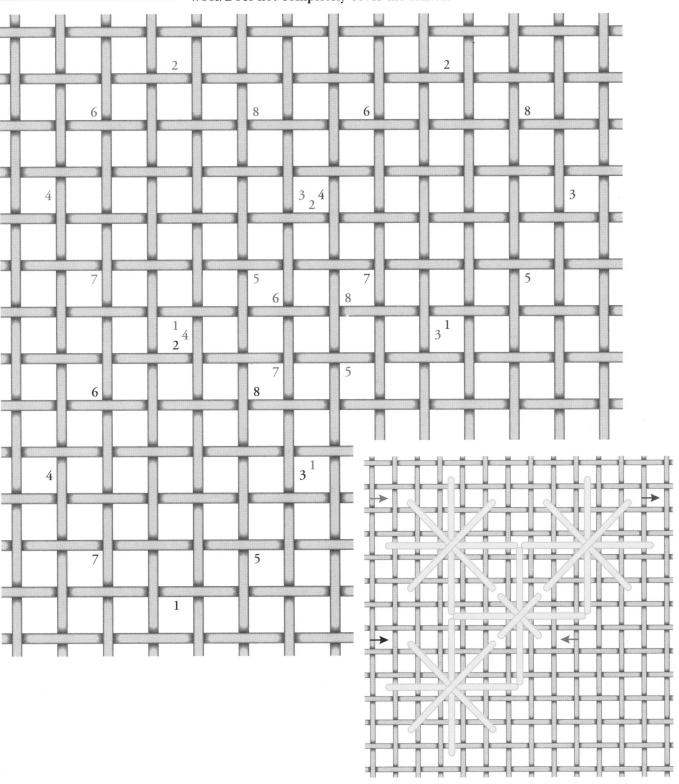

Elongated Smyrna Cross

Worked on monofil in horizontal rows. You first do a
diagonal cross (1-2-3-4). Then you make a second
cross on top of the first one (5-6-7-8). This stitch
makes a lovely border.

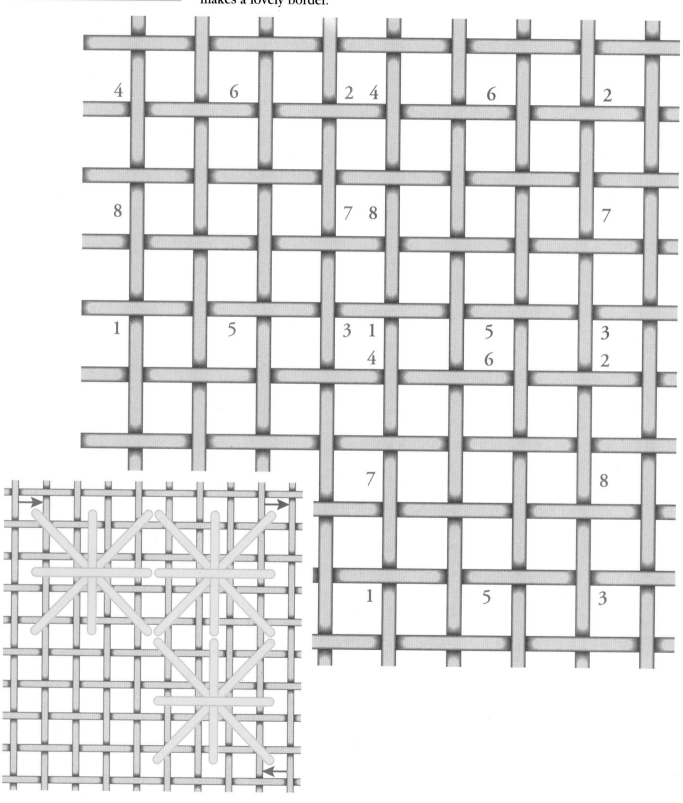

Reversed Elongated Smyrna Cross 14

Worked on monofil in horizontal rows. Make a diagonal cross, then a straight cross over it. Reverse the order in the next stitch: straight cross, then diagonal cross. You can use two colors or two tones of the same color. On second row, stitch the cross contrariwise to the one above. Use thick wool. Does not completely cover canvas.

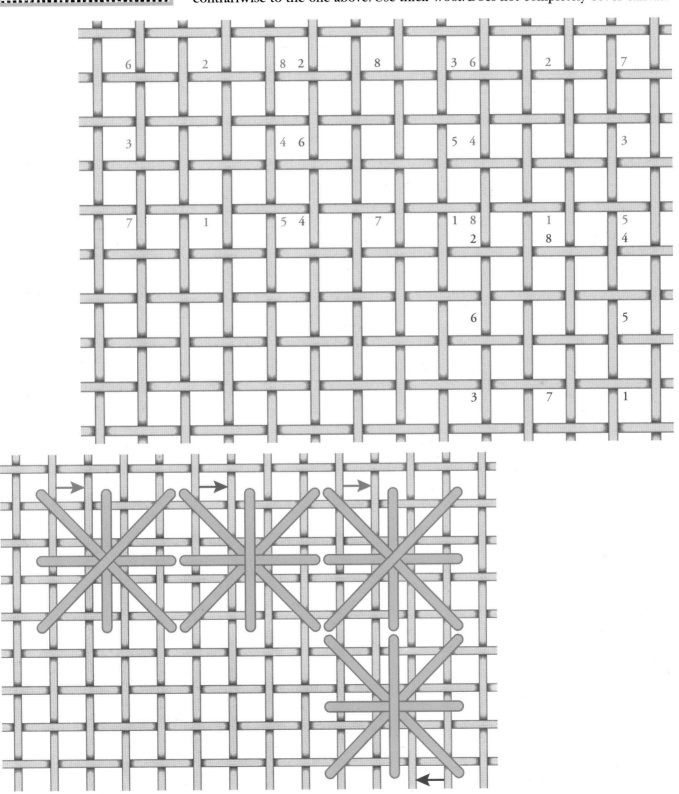

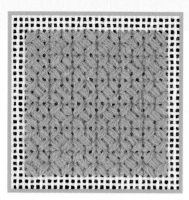

Long Rice

Worked on monofil in horizontal rows. Use thick wool. First make a diagonal cross, then cover each cross point. Covers the canvas well.

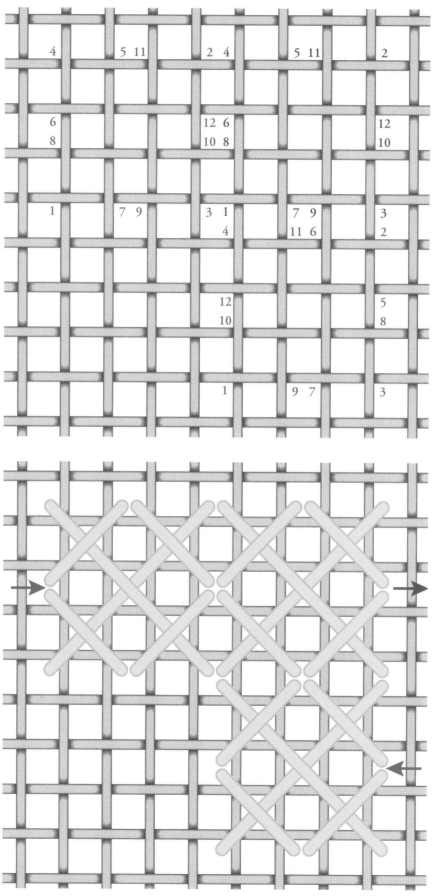

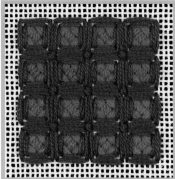

Framed Long Rice

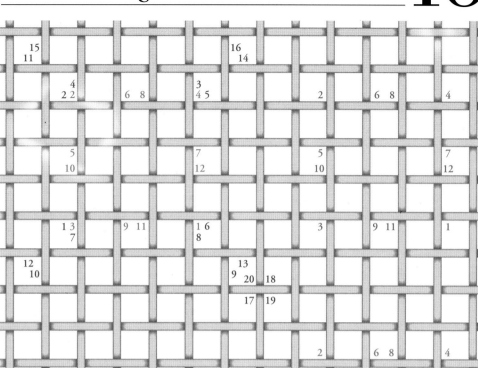

Worked on monofil in horizontal rows, in two sections. Use thick wool. First work the squares (long rice stitch), then work the double frame and the cross stitch in another color. Covers the canvas fairly well.

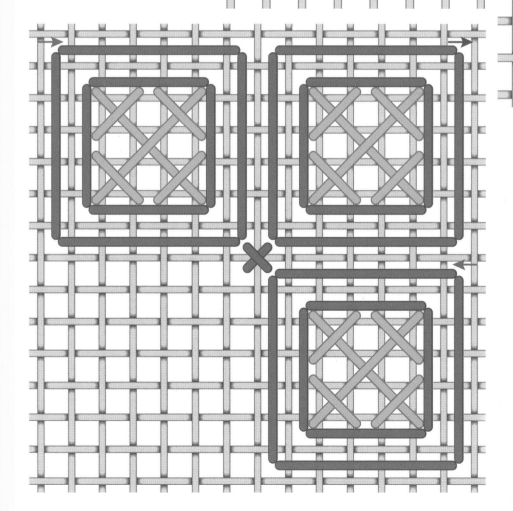

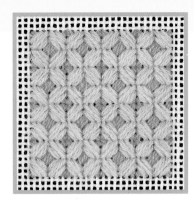

Triple Rice

Worked on monofil in horizontal rows, in two separate steps. Two colors. Work the first big crosses with a thicker thread than the finishing stitches. Though the mauve numbers indicate how to work the whole figure all at once, it is easier to first finish the top half of the row, then finish the bottom half in a second pass. Covers the canvas well.

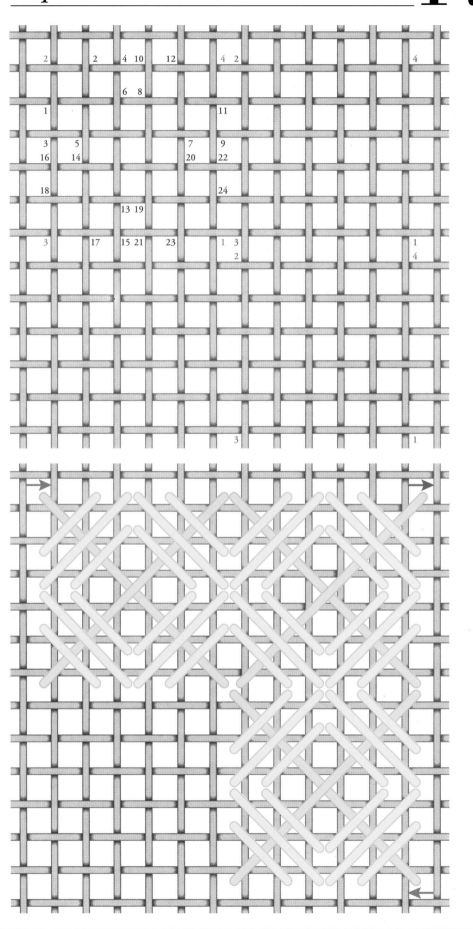

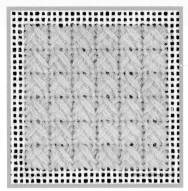

Braided Diagonal Cross

Worked on monofil in horizontal rows. Medium wool thickness. Covers the canvas well.

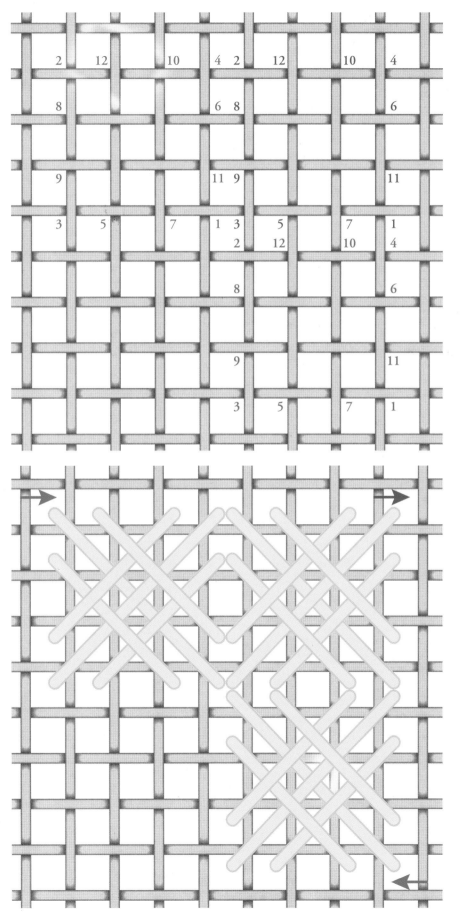

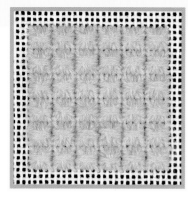

Double Leviathan

Worked on monofil either in horizontal or vertical rows, or even in diagonal rows if you are using alternating colors. Medium wool thickness. Covers the canvas well.

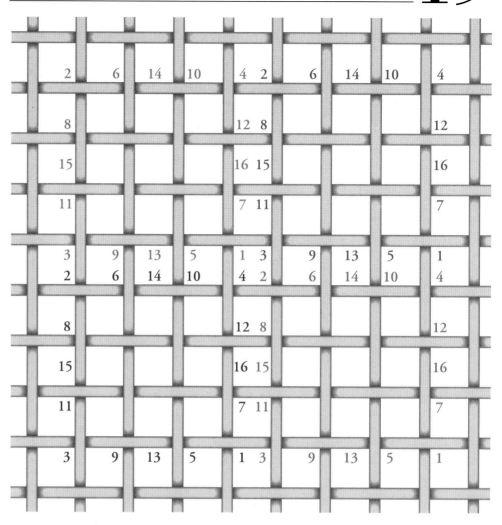

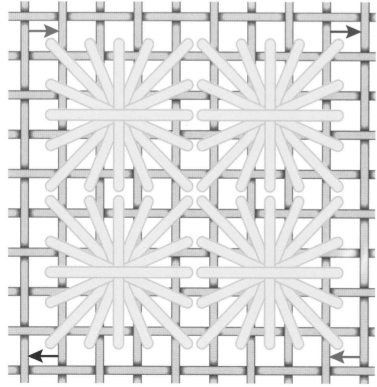

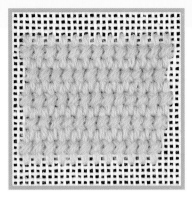

Crossed Gobelin

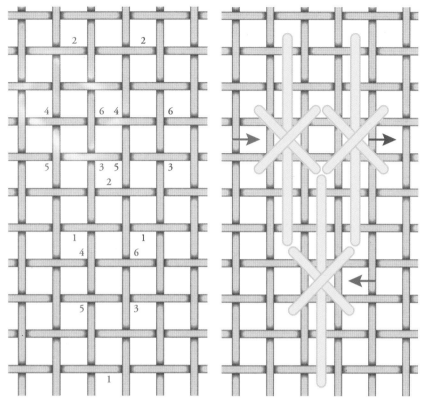

Worked on monofil in horizontal rows. This is a long Gobelin stitch with a cross in the middle. The second row is offset from the first. Use thick thread. Covers canvas well.

Oblong Cross

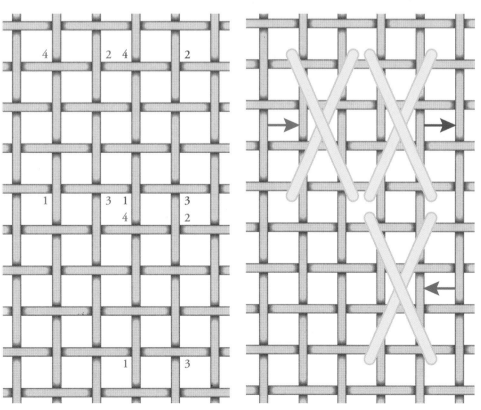

Can be worked on monofil or penelope, in horizontal rows. Thick wool. Does not cover canvas completely.

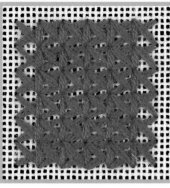

Montenegro Cross

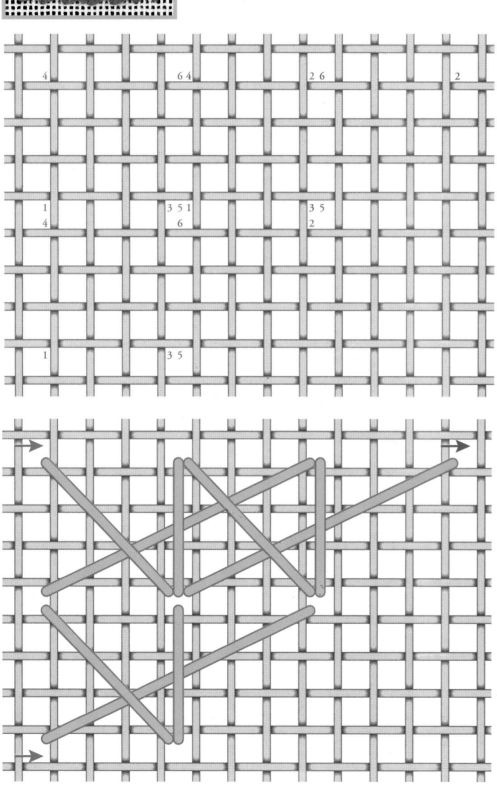

Worked on monofil in horizontal rows, always from left to right. Use very thick thread. This stitch is long and fairly loose and does not cover the canvas well.

Tressed Stitch

23

Worked on monofil. Very thick wool.
This stitch does not cover canvas well.

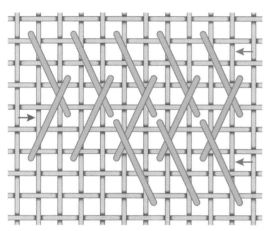

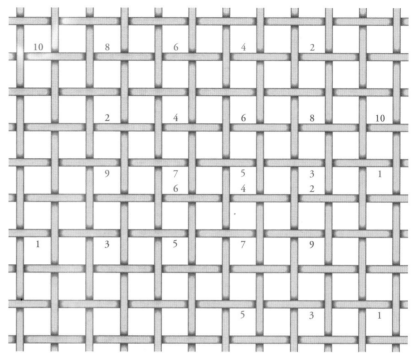

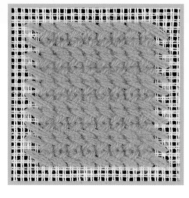

Greek Stitch

24

Worked in horizontal rows, from left to right only, on penelope canvas. Terminate your needleful at the end of each row and start over on the left. Only use thick wool. Does not entirely cover the canvas.

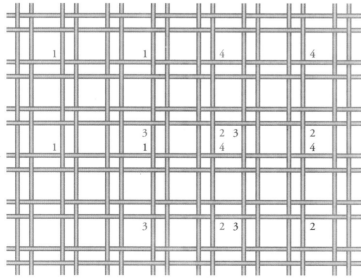

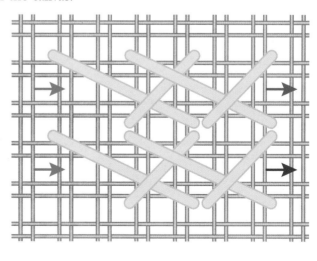

Long Plaited Stitch

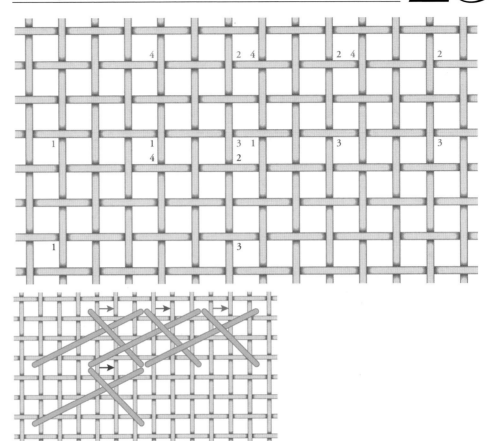

Worked on monofil in horizontal rows, from left to right only. At the end of each row, stop your needleful and start over at the left. Very thick wool thread. Does not cover canvas well.

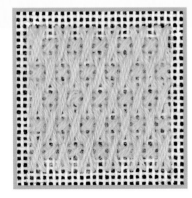

Double Stitch

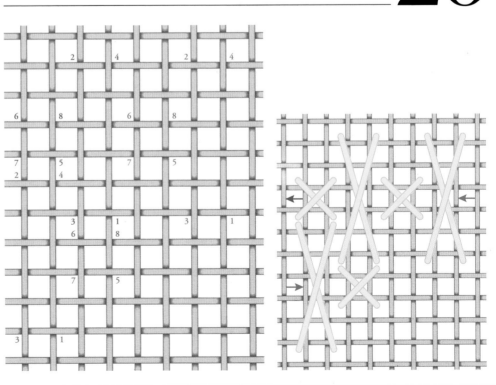

Worked on monofil in horizontal rows. Thick wool thread. Does not cover canvas completely.

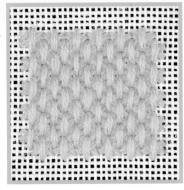

Dutch Stitch

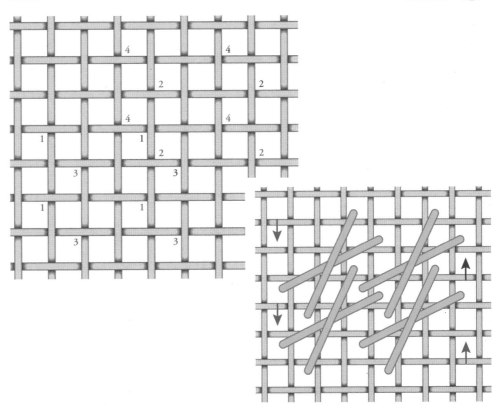

Worked on monofil in horizontal rows. Thick wool thread. Covers canvas fairly well. Second row is offset from first row.

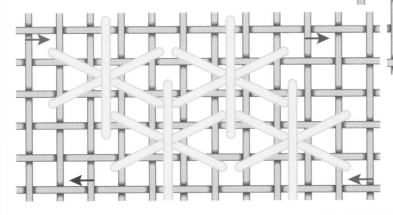

Labor Stitch

Worked on monofil in vertical rows. Thick wool thread. Does not cover canvas well.

Spanish Stitch

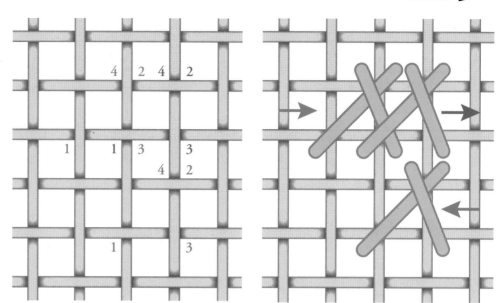

Worked on monofil in horizontal rows. Fairly thick thread. Covers canvas well.

Algerian Braided Stitch

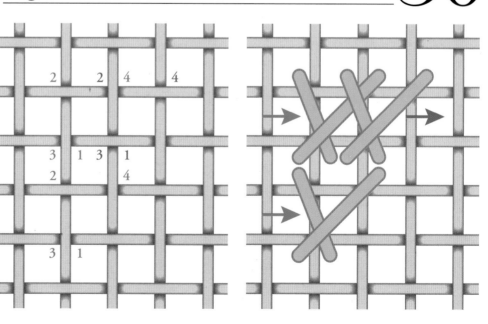

This stitch resembles the Spanish stitch. It is worked on monofil canvas in horizontal rows. Use a medium thick thread. Covers canvas fairly well. Always work from left to right. Terminate your needleful at the end of each row and start over at the left.

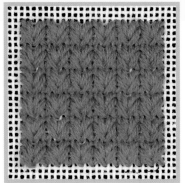

Branched Cross Stitch

Worked on monofil in horizontal or vertical rows. Use thick wool thread. Covers the canvas fairly well.

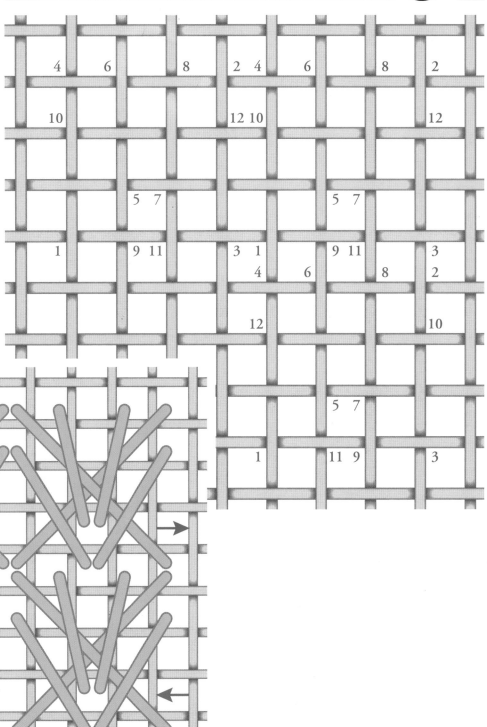

Worked on monofil. Very thick thread. Covers canvas well. Terminate your needleful at the end of each row and start over on the left.

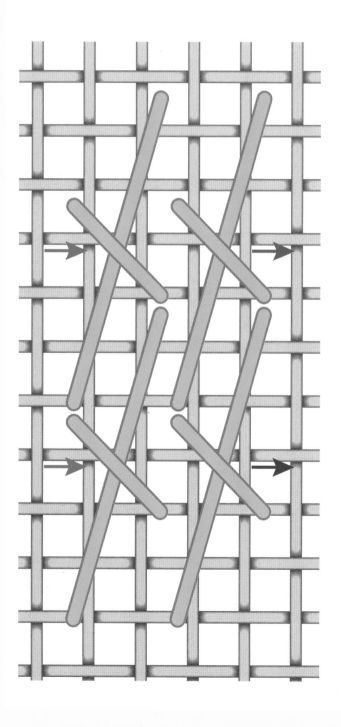

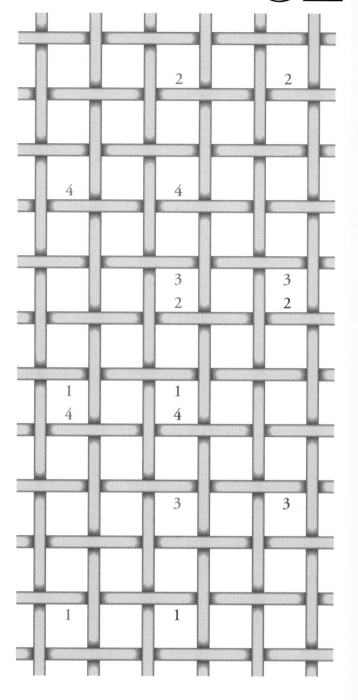

Fern Stitch

Worked on monofil canvas in vertical rows. Medium wool thickness. Covers the canvas well. When you get to the bottom of the row, terminate your needleful and start over at the top.

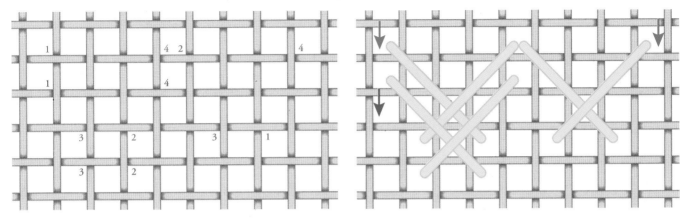

Plaited Stitch

Worked on monofil in vertical rows. Thin wool thread. Covers canvas very well. A very lovely stitch. A bit fastidious to work.

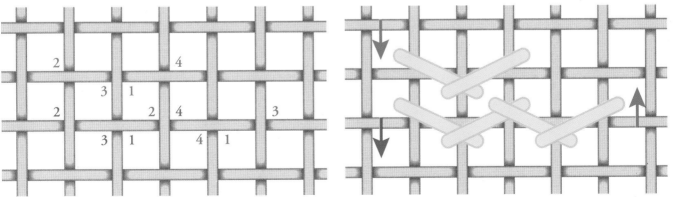

Long and Short Oblique

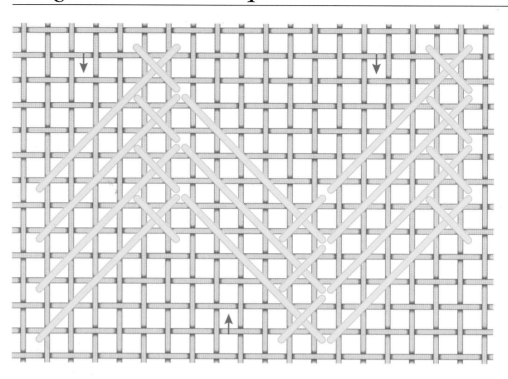

Worked in vertical rows on
monofil. Very thick thread.
Covers the canvas pretty well.

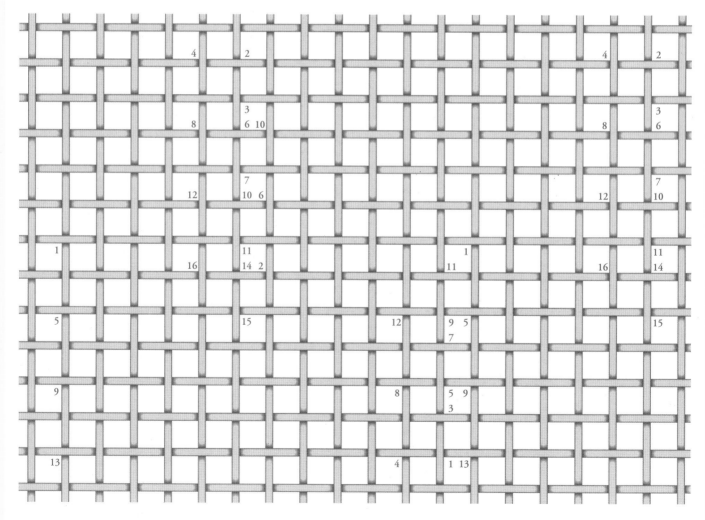

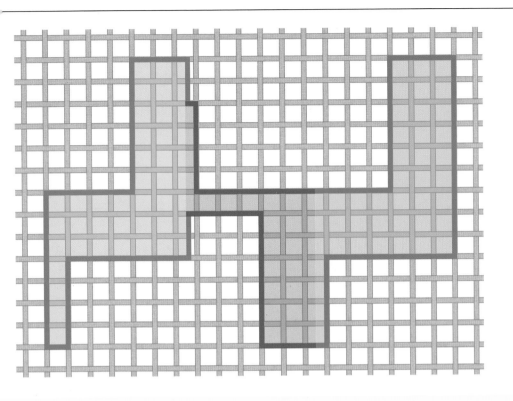

Herringbone Stitch (Variation)

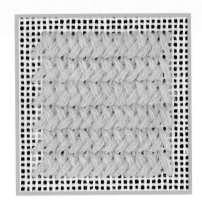

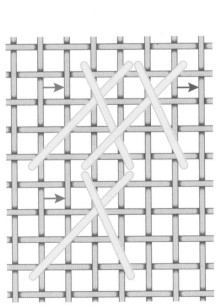

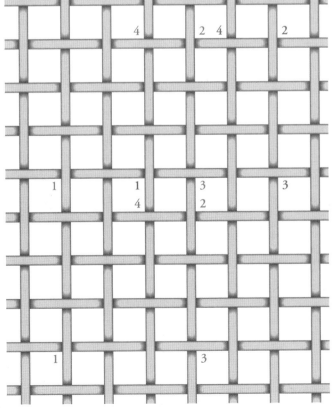

Worked on monofil or penelope in horizontal rows, from left to right. Stop at end of row, start over at beginning of next row. Very thick thread. Covers canvas well.

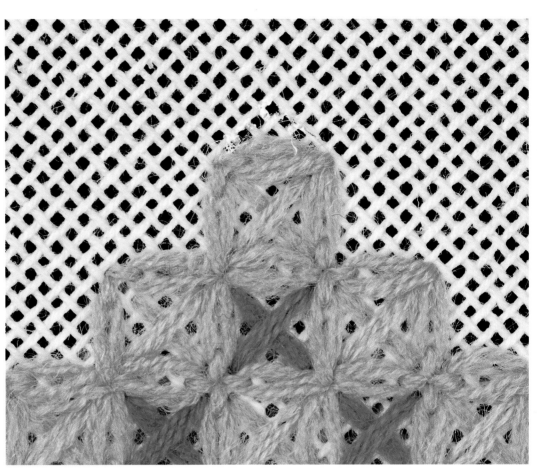

THE LOOPED STITCHES

Chain Stitch

Worked on penelope with thin wool thread. Stitched in vertical rows. Covers the canvas well.

Come out at 1, go in at 2, hold the loop, come out at 3 inside the loop, pull, hold the thread to form the second loop, go in at 4 on the outside of the first loop, etc. End the last stitch by pushing the needle on the outside of the loop in the same hole.

Turn the canvas upside down to start over, or stop your needleful and start over next to the first stitch without turning the canvas.

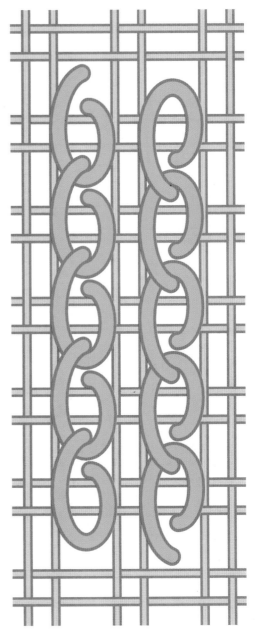

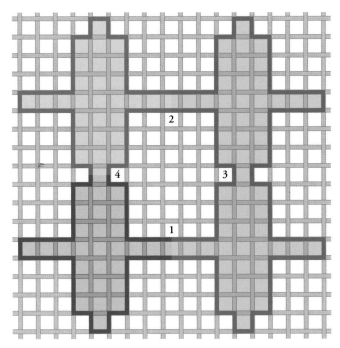

Detached Chain Stitch

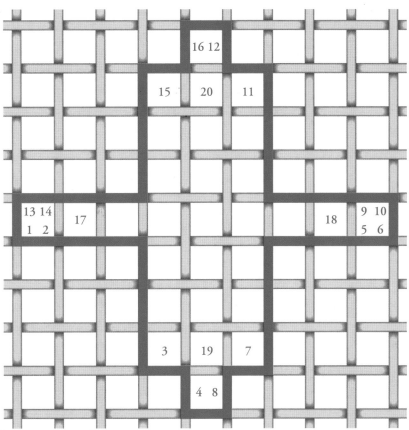

Stitched on monofil in horizontal or vertical rows. Very thick wool thread. Does not cover the canvas well.

Come out at 1 and go back into the same hole at 2, forming a loop. Do not pull. Take the needle out at 3, go through the loop with the needle, and insert the needle at 4. Be careful that the loop is well formed, with the wool straight and full and the loop even. Use the same procedure for the other three loops. In the center, stitch a cross (17-18-19-20).

In the center of four figures, work a cross (marked 1-2-3-4 on the diagram below). In the photo, the center cross is shown in red.

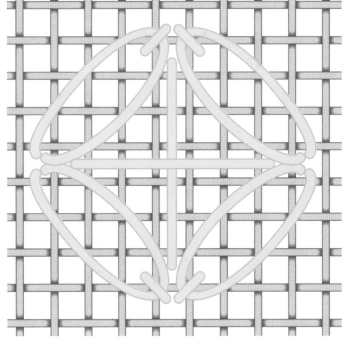

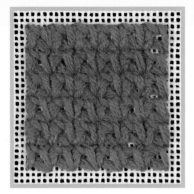

Eastern Stitch

Worked on monofil in horizontal rows. Very thick thread. Does not cover the canvas well. Follow the numbers to 6. At 6-7, pass the needle under stitches 3-4 without going into the canvas. Do the same for 8-9 and push your needle in at 10. Keep a loose tension on the thread in order to leave the canvas as well covered as possible.

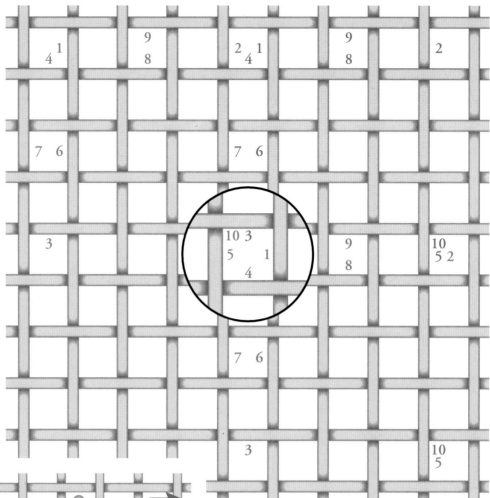

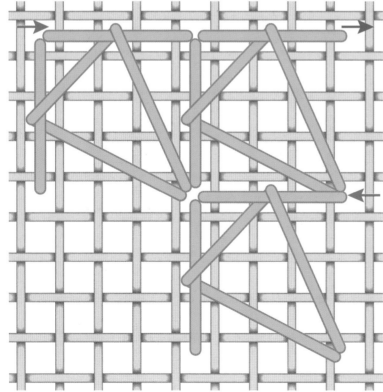

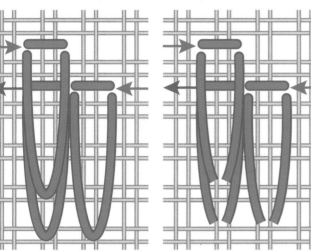

Cut Turkey Work

This is a fringe worked on penelope. You can make a single row or several rows, working from the bottom up. The circled numbers show the stitches that form the loop. As you finish each row, cut the loops with fine scissors. (Photo shows a partially cut row.) Trim the fringe when you finish, of course.

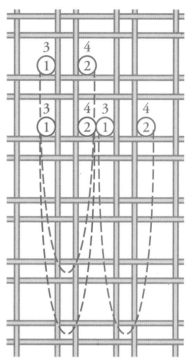

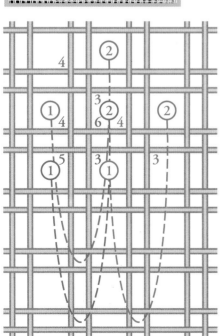

Velvet Stitch

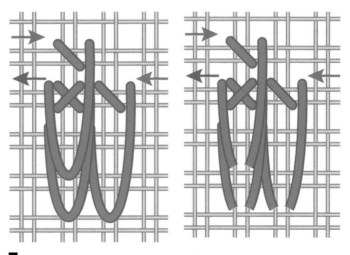

This stitch is the one used to make rugs. It is worked on penelope in horizontal rows from the bottom up. On the diagram, the dashed lines indicate the loose loops. At the end of the first row, the 5-6 is an added stitch that allows you to start the second row, above (the green number 1).

As you finish each row, you will cut the loops with fine scissors.

Once the work is finished, you can trim the cut loops short so that the surface looks like velvet, or you can leave them long. The texture is very, very thick.

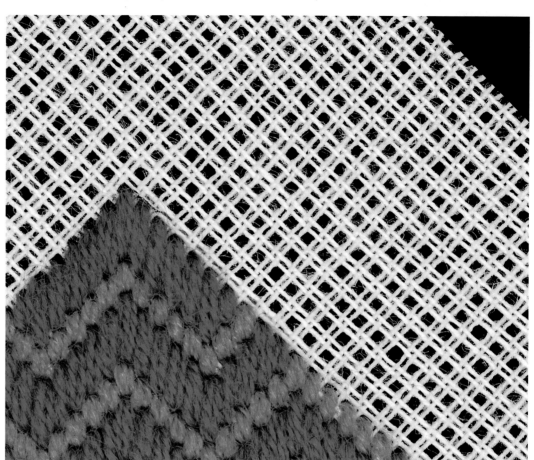

THE LONG STITCHES

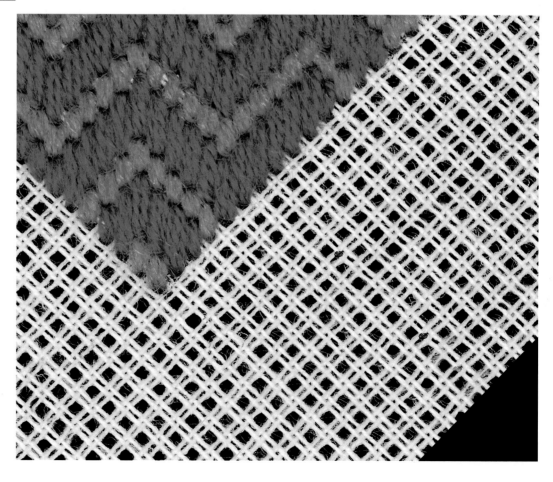

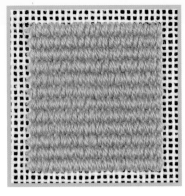

Renaissance Stitch

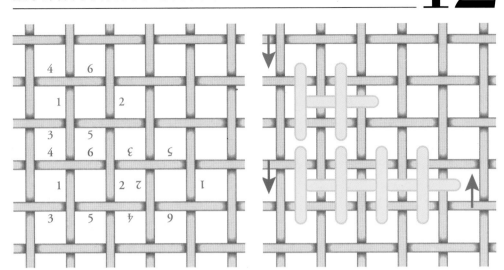

Use monofil canvas only. Thin wool thread. Worked in vertical rows. Turn the canvas at the end of each row and start over in the opposite direction.

Tramèd Continental Stitch

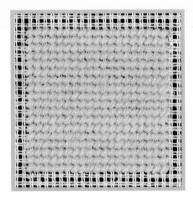

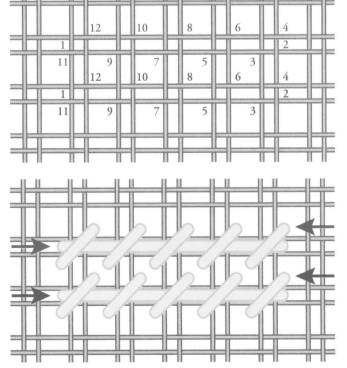

Worked only on penelope. The tramé (the long horizontal thread) is always stitched from left to right. Never do the continental stitch without the tramé. If you tried, on the left-to-right rows you would be doing the half-cross stitch, which is never used by serious needlepointers because it leaves the back of the canvas bare. If you do not want to tramé the continental stitch, you must end your needleful and start over on the right-hand side each time.

Use a medium thickness thread. Covers the canvas very well. This stitch is practical for counted stitchwork.

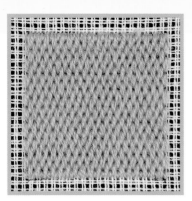

Brick Stitch

Worked on penelope canvas. Medium wool thickness. This is a lovely stitch and is often used for background. Covers the canvas very well.

Mosaic Stitch

Worked on monofil in diagonal rows. Medium thick wool. Covers canvas well.

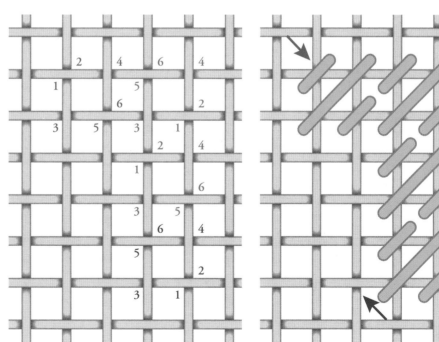

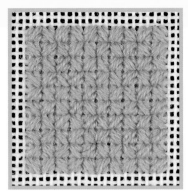

Reversed Mosaic Stitch

Worked on monofil in
diagonal rows. The stitches
of the second row are the
reverse of those of the first
row. Medium wool thickness.
Covers the canvas well.

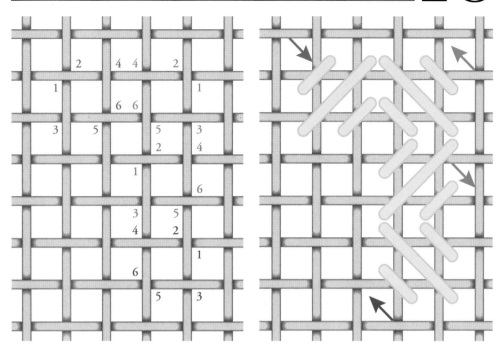

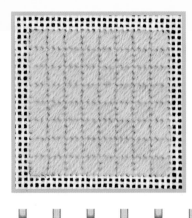

Scotch Stitch

Worked on monofil in
diagonal rows. Medium
thread thickness.
Covers canvas well.

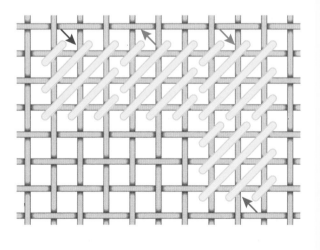

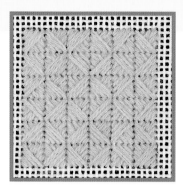

Worked on monofil in vertical, horizontal, or diagonal rows. Use a medium thread thickness. Covers canvas well.

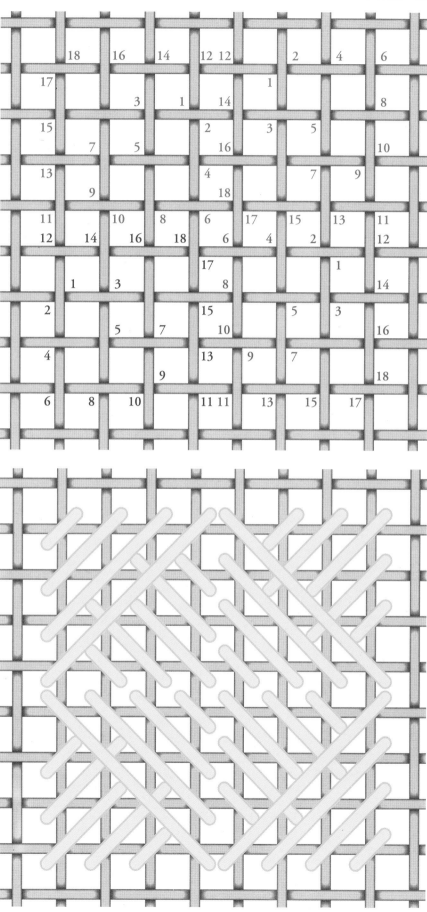

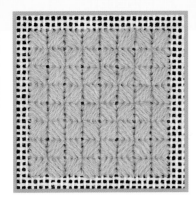

Reversed Scotch Stitch

Worked on monofil canvas in diagonal rows. Medium wool thickness. Covers the canvas well.

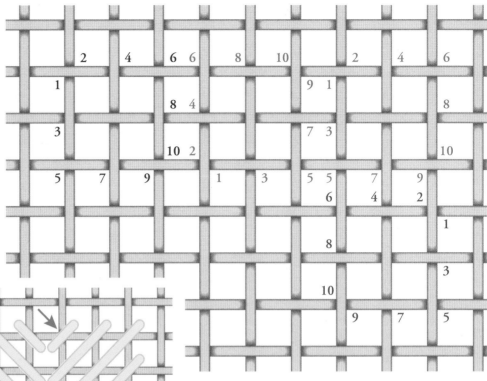

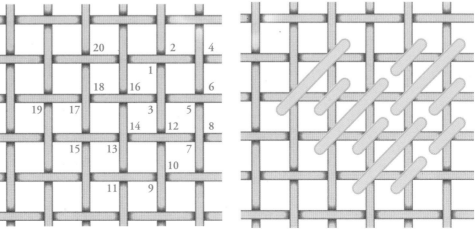

Diagonal Mosaic Stitch

Worked on monofil in diagonal rows. Medium wool thickness. A very nice background stitch, especially if design is done in basketweave.

Cashmere Stitch

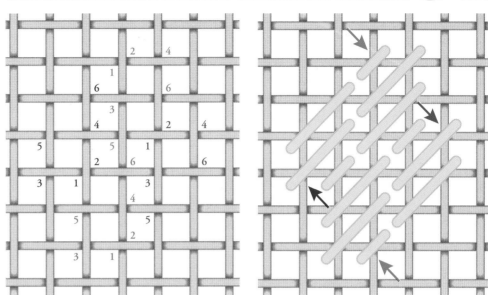

Stitched in monofil. Medium thread thickness. Covers the canvas very well.

Straight Cashmere Stitch

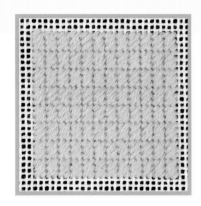

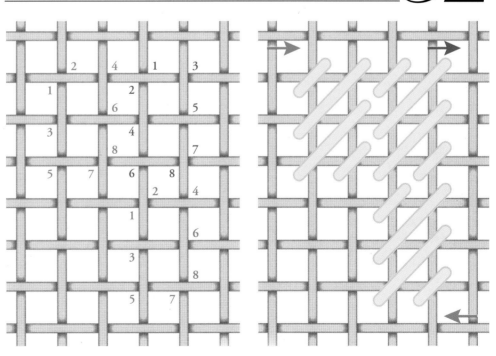

Worked in either horizontal or vertical rows. On the diagrams, the numbers are reversed from row to row to avoid pushing the needle up through spaces already stitched.

Medium thread thickness. Covers canvas very well and makes a lovely background.

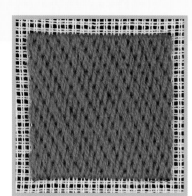

Woven Stitch

Stitched on penelope canvas in diagonal rows. Start at the top left. At the end of the row, which is very steep, turn the canvas around and start the second row. At the end of each row turn the canvas.

Medium thread thickness. Covers the canvas well.

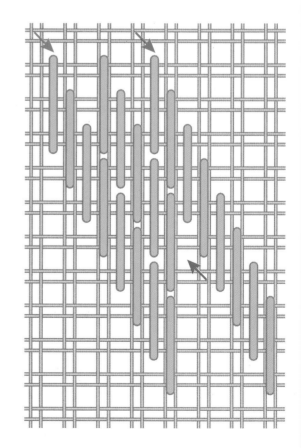

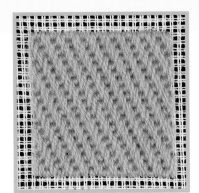

Double Woven Stitch

Stitched on penelope canvas in diagonal rows. Medium thread thickness. Covers the canvas very well.

Make straight stitches over three meshes, starting at top left and going down diagonally. At the end of the row, turn the canvas and start the second row underneath the first row, this time stitching over one mesh. At the end of each row, turn the canvas.

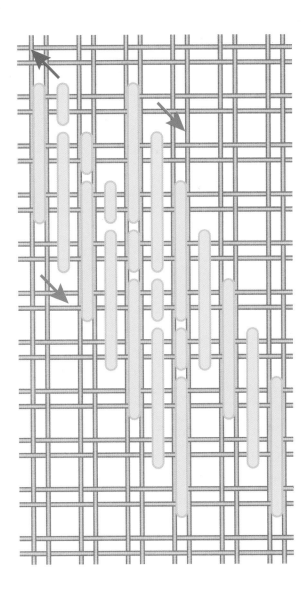

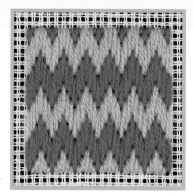

Straight Stitch, Bargello Style

Most attractive when stitched on penelope. This stitch can also be worked on monofil, but it will have a different look. Note that on monofil the stitch is less tight (see diagram and photo on next page), therefore the wool should be thicker.

You can work this stitch in one or several colors. You can let your imagination run. Stitch over four meshes, in horizontal rows, from left to right and right to left, depending on the color.

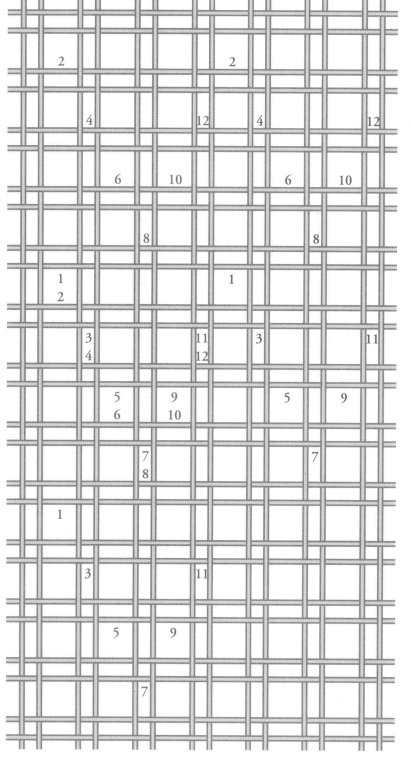

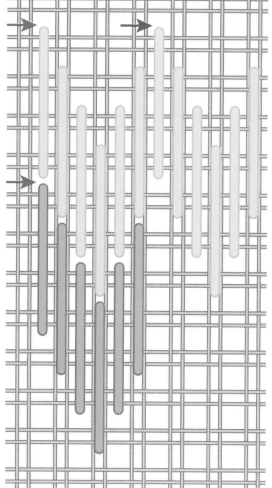

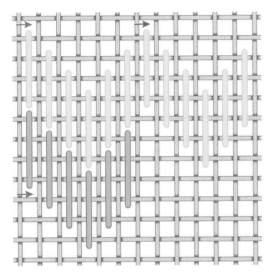

Straight Stitch, Bargello Style, on monofil canvas

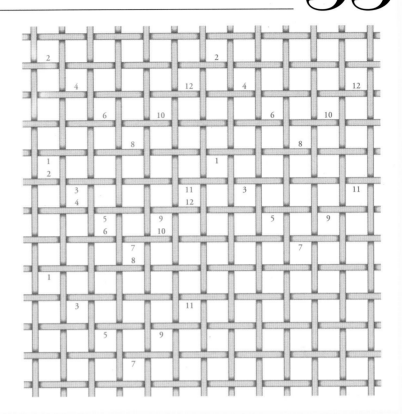

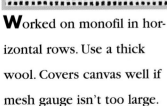

Hungarian Stitch

the second and fourth rows.

On the diagram, the mauve numbers show the beginning of the third row, if you are working with a single color.

Worked on monofil in horizontal rows. Use a thick wool. Covers canvas well if mesh gauge isn't too large.

Leave the needleful at the end of the first row, if it is a different color from the second row. You will pick up the needle to work the third row (from right to left) after finishing the second row. Do the same with

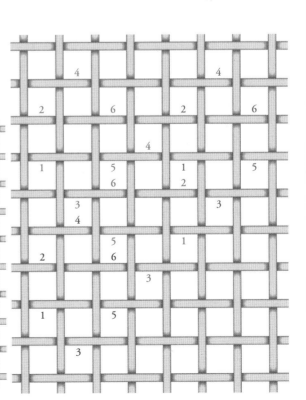

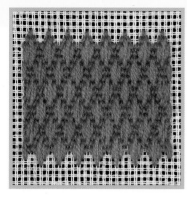

Framed Hungarian Stitch

Worked on penelope in horizontal rows.
Use a medium thick wool thread. Covers
the canvas well. You can use several colors
and create different designs.

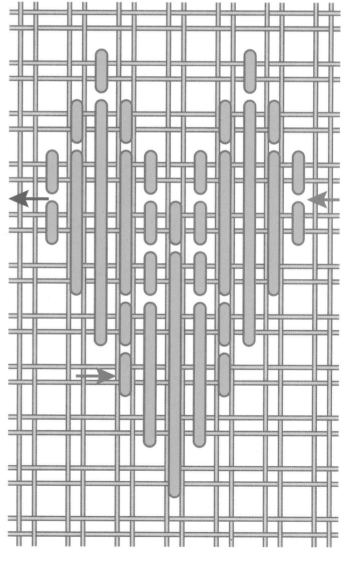

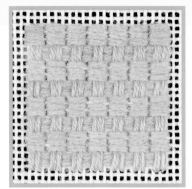

Pavement Stitch

58

Stitched on monofil canvas. This stitch is reminiscent of pavement or wicker.

Work in horizontal rows using fairly thick wool thread. Covers the canvas well.

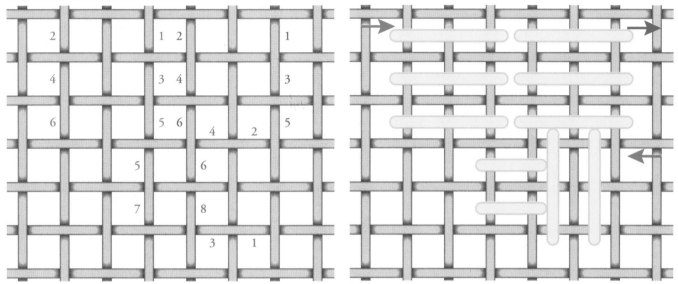

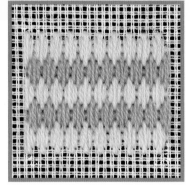

Straight Stitch, Florentine Style

59

Use penelope canvas; the effect is more elegant than if it were stitched on monofil. The second row can be of a different color or a different hue. You can go from right to left, or from left to right.

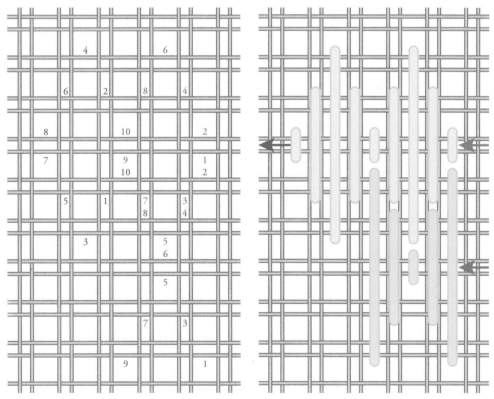

Scotch Checkerboard

Stitched on monofil in horizontal or vertical rows. Start at the top right and make a square with basketweave, a second with diagonal stitches, etc. Medium thickness of wool. Covers the canvas well.

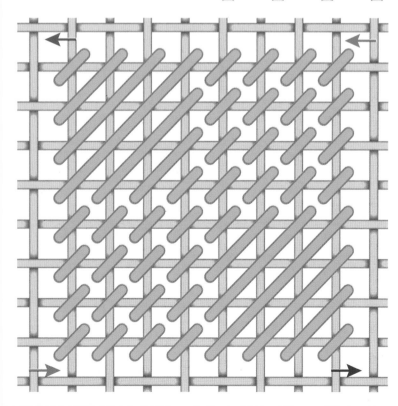

Framed Scotch Stitch

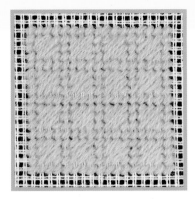

Stitched on penelope in vertical or horizontal rows. Can be stitched on monofil but always keep in mind that a minimum of two canvas threads must be covered with each stitch, which will take some acrobatics on monofil. Use fairly thick thread. Covers the canvas well.

2	4	8	14	20					
1	3 6	7 10	13 16	19 22	26				
5	9 12		25 28	32					
11	15 18		31 34	38					
17	21 24	27 30	33 36	37 40	42	31	29	25	21
23	29 2	35 4	39 8	41 12	32 16	30 27	26 23	22 19	17
1	3 6		15 18	28 22				18 15	11
5	7 10		21 24	24 28				12 9	5
9	11 14	17 20	23 26	27 30	20 32	16 13	10 7	6 3	1
13	19	25	29	31	14	8	4	2	

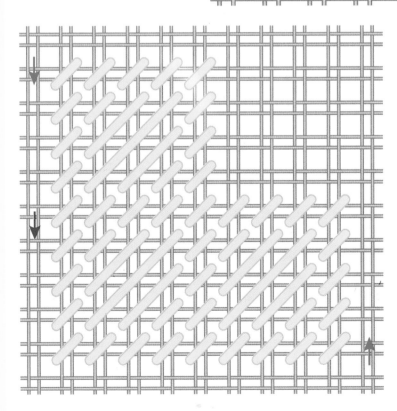

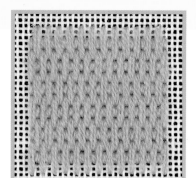

Parisian Stitch

Stitched on monofil in horizontal rows. The second row is offset from the first. Medium wool thread thickness. Covers the canvas well.

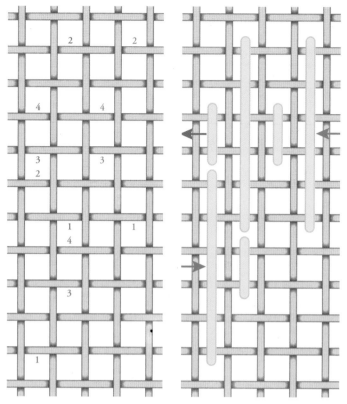

Linen Stitch

Worked on penelope canvas. It can also be done on monofil but is prettier on penelope. Worked in diagonal rows. Medium wool thread thickness. Covers the canvas well. This stitch imitates the reverse side of basketweave (see p. 21) but does not have its thickness.

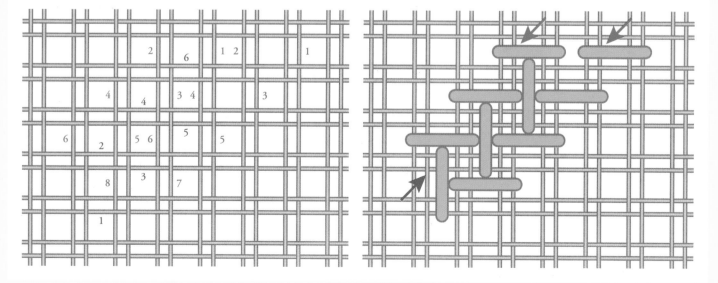

Triangle Stitch

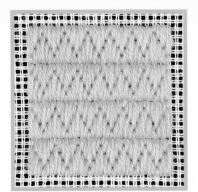

Stitched on penelope canvas. Medium wool thread thickness. Covers the canvas well. These rows of triangles make good borders.

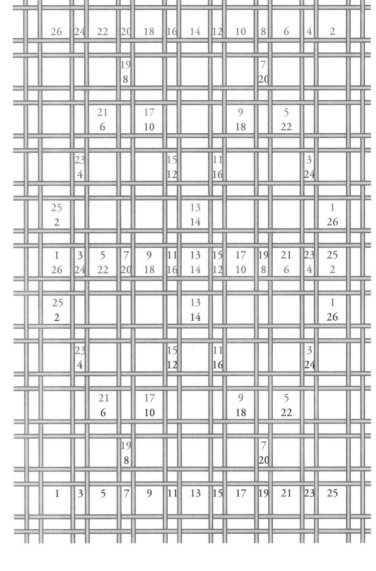

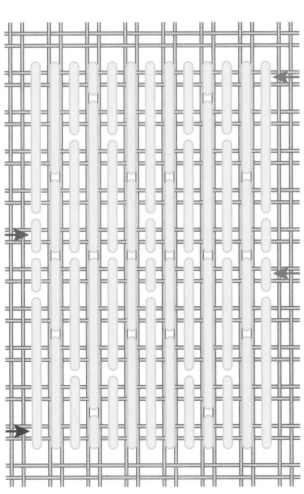

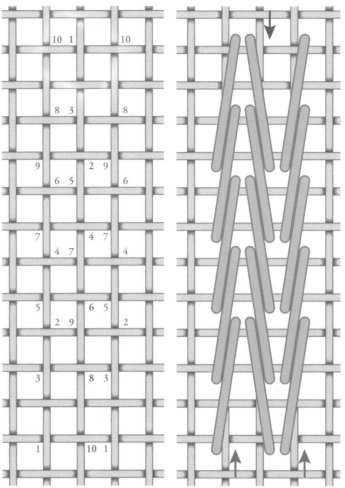

Stitched on monofil canvas in vertical rows. Use thick wool thread. Covers canvas pretty well.

Be sure to pull the thread very evenly, otherwise it will have a slovenly appearance.

Cloth Stitch
66

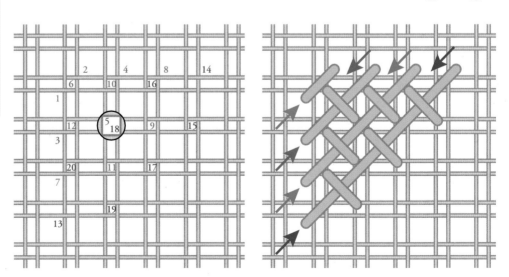

Work on penelope only. Long diagonal stitches are crossed by stitches worked using only the small holes. It is important to follow the number indications carefully.

Use a thin wool thread. Covers the canvas fairly well.

Best used only for very small areas because of the difficulty of execution; however, it is a very handsome stitch.

Jacquard Stitch

Worked on penelope canvas.

Long diagonal stitches in a

zigzag pattern.

   Use thick wool thread.

Covers canvas fairly well.

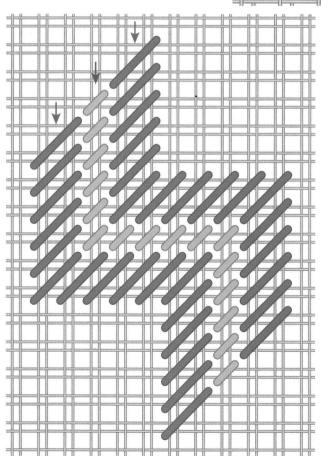

Jacquard Stitch—Variation

Stitched on monofil. Long stitches worked diagonally in zigzag rows. Use thick wool thread. Covers the canvas well.

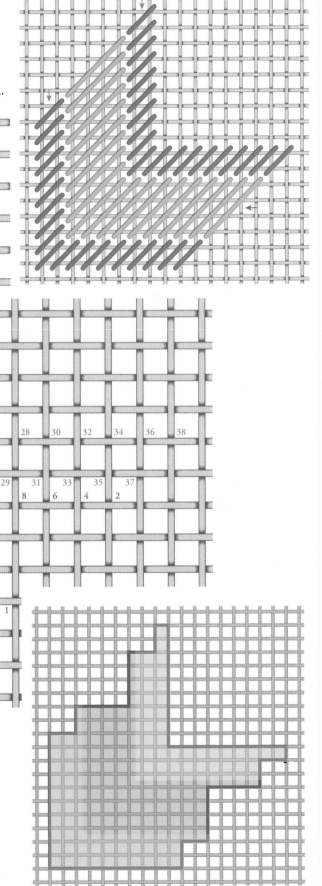

Byzantine Stitch

Stitched on monofil. This stitch, like many of the Jacquard-type stitches, can be worked on different mesh counts and in different colors. Use thick thread. Covers the canvas well.

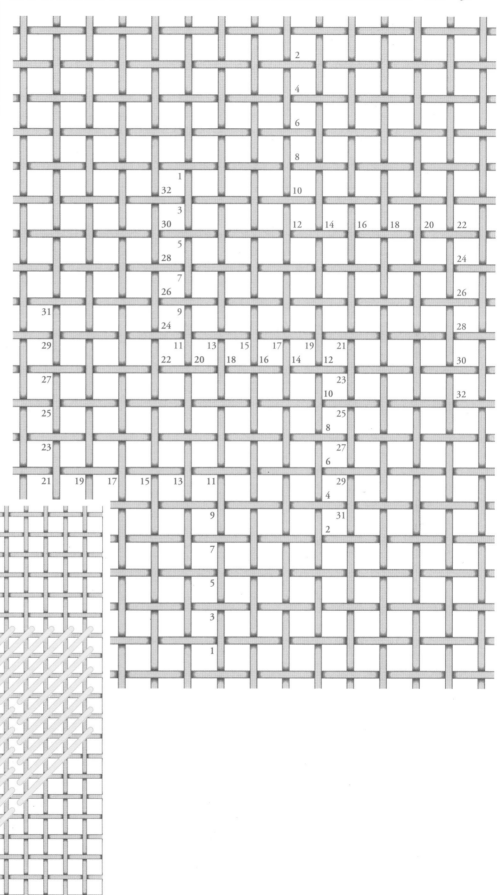

70

Oblique Slav Stitch

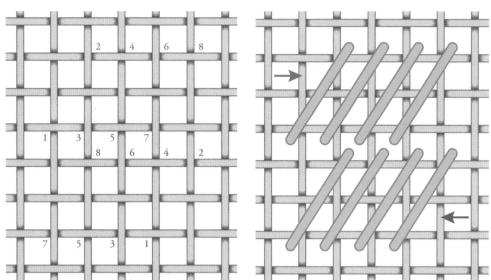

Worked on monofil canvas in horizontal rows. Covers canvas fairly well. Use thick thread.

71

Moorish Stitch

Worked on monofil in diagonal rows. Use thick thread. Covers canvas pretty well. This is a lovely background stitch.

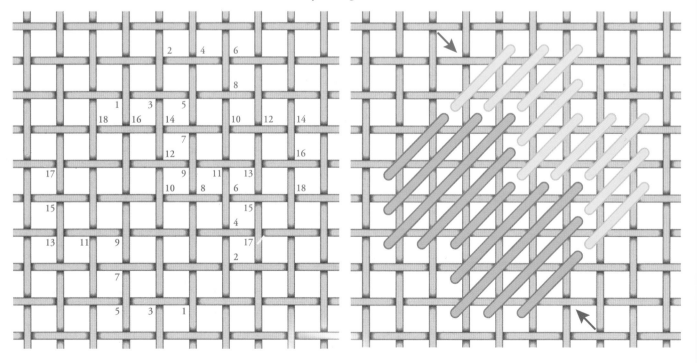

Interlocking Stitch

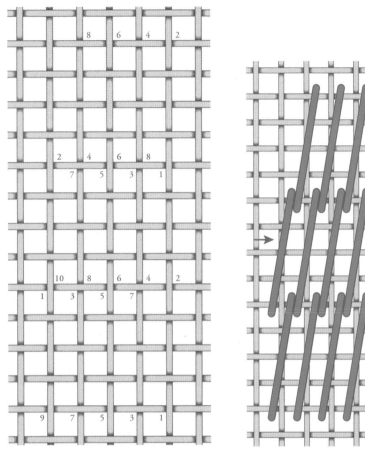

Worked on monofil in horizontal rows. Use thick thread. Covers canvas fairly well.

Do not try to economize on wool (see p. 36); the double thickness front and back creates the richness of its look.

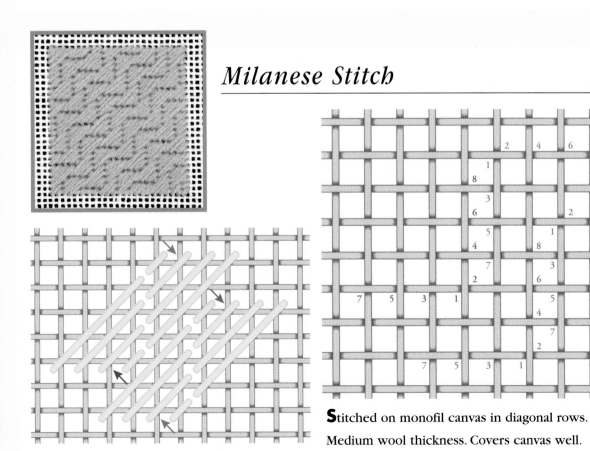

Milanese Stitch

Stitched on monofil canvas in diagonal rows. Medium wool thickness. Covers canvas well.

Oriental Stitch

Worked on monofil canvas in diagonal rows. You can turn the canvas at the end of each row, or work each row without turning the canvas if you don't get confused. Medium wool thread thickness. Covers the canvas well.

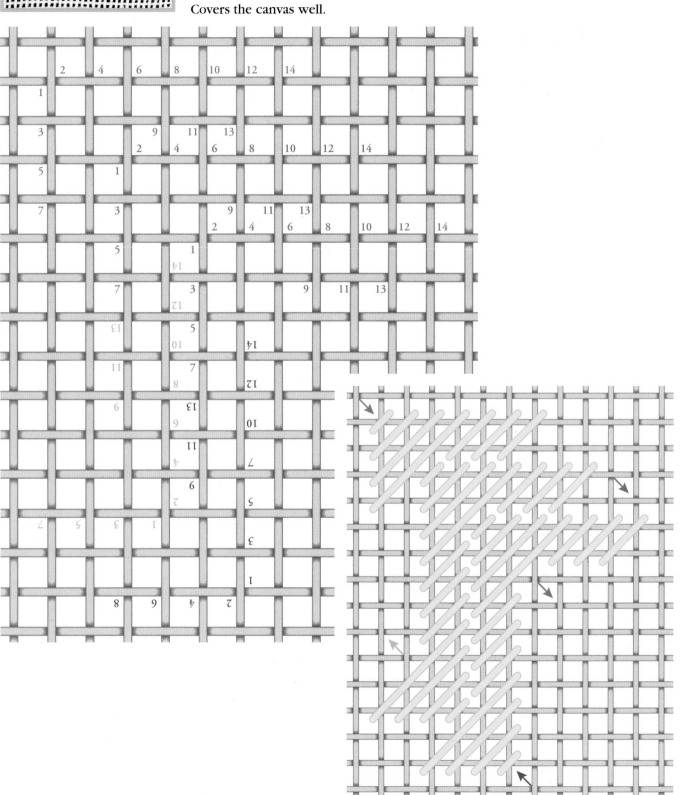

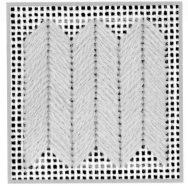

Branch Stitch

Stitched on monofil canvas. Very thick wool thread. Worked in vertical rows. Covers canvas fairly well.

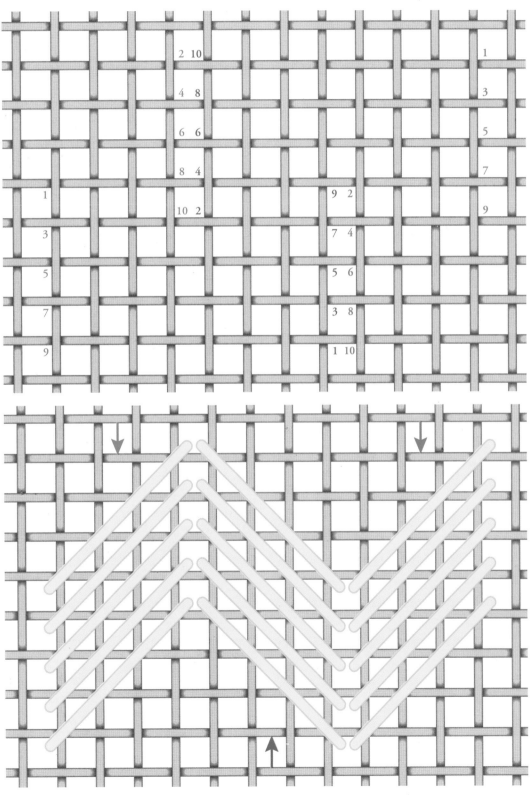

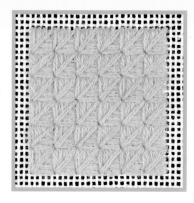

Leaf Stitch

Stitched on monofil canvas in horizontal rows. This is a fast stitch to work. Use thick wool thread. Covers canvas fairly well.

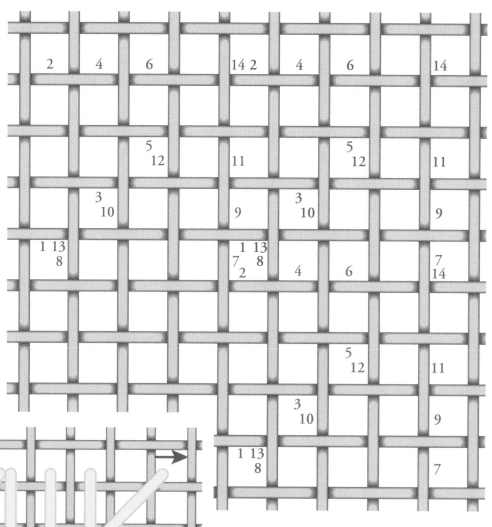

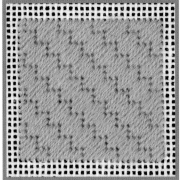

Diagonal Hexagonal Stitch

Stitched on monofil canvas. Medium thread thickness. Covers canvas very well. On a fine canvas, this stitch makes a lovely background.

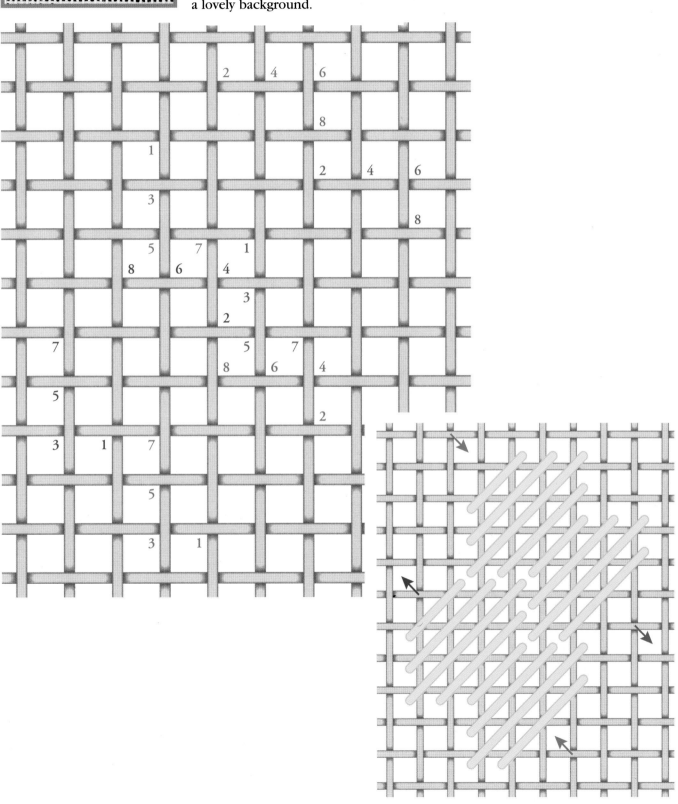

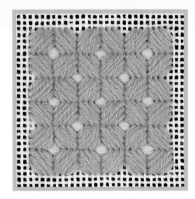

Brighton Stitch

Worked on monofil canvas in horizontal rows, in two steps and two colors. Once the squares are finished, make a cross in the center of each. Use thick wool thread. Covers canvas fairly well.

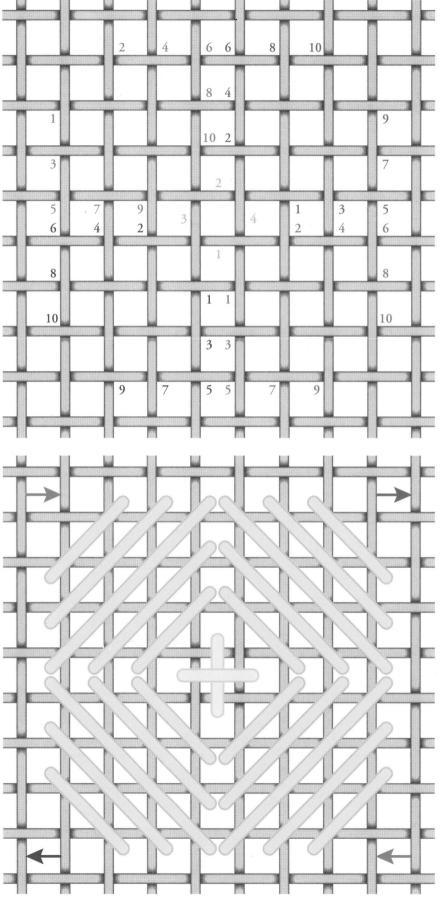

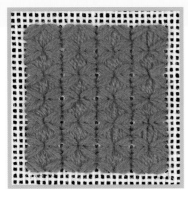

English Stitch

Stitched on monofil canvas in horizontal rows. Use fairly thick thread. Covers the canvas fairly well.

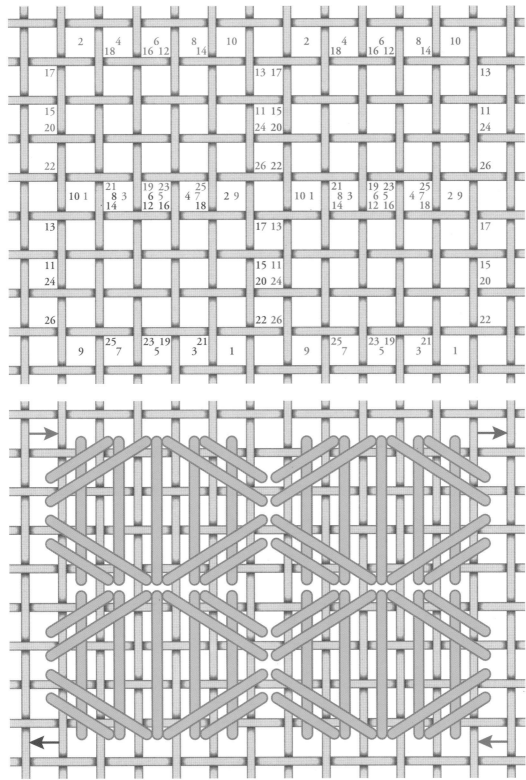

Pineapple Stitch

Worked on monofil canvas in horizontal rows. Medium thread thickness. Some canvas shows.

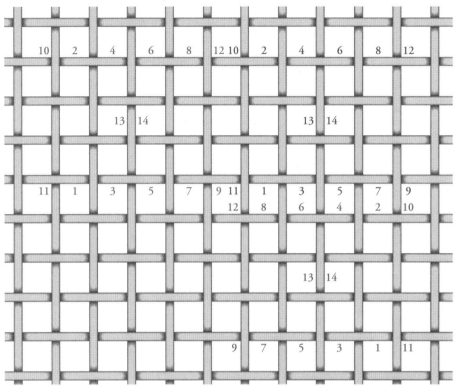

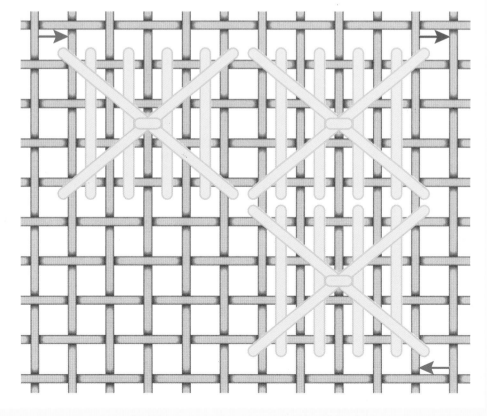

Perspective Stitch

Stitched on monofil canvas
in horizontal or vertical
rows, in two colors. Medium
thread thickness. Covers the
canvas fairly well.

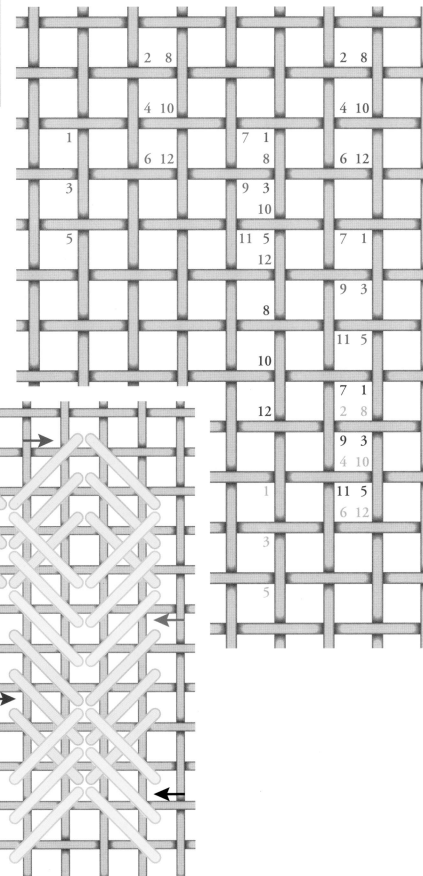

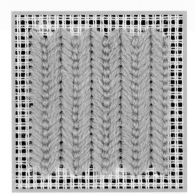

Stem Stitch

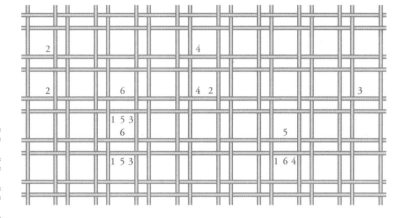

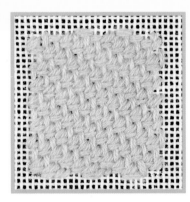

Stitched on penelope in vertical rows. Medium thickness wool thread. Covers the canvas well.

Easel Stitch

Worked on monofil in diagonal rows, always in the same direction, from the left down. Start working at top right; following rows start at the left of the preceding row. Terminate your needleful when you get to the bottom and start over on top. Covers canvas fairly well.

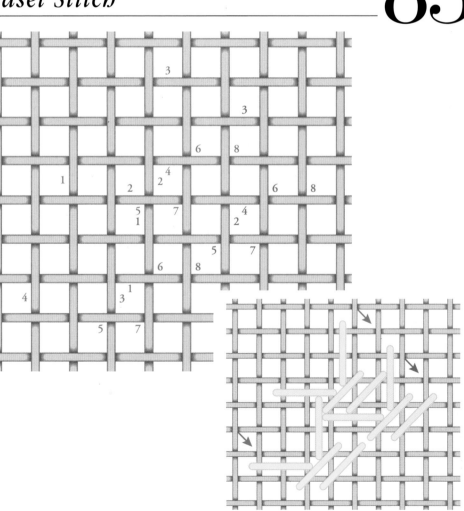

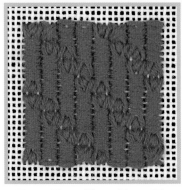

Bobbin Stitch

Stitched on monofil canvas in diagonal rows. Medium thread thickness. Covers canvas fairly well.

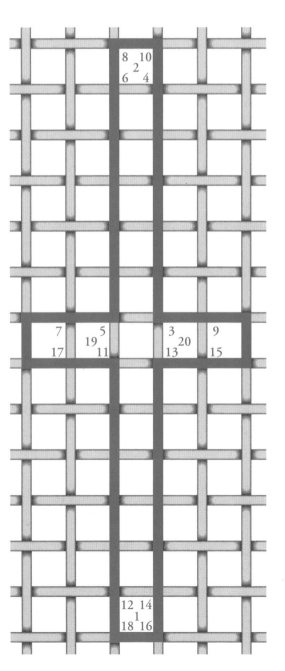

Umbrella Stitch

Stitched on monofil canvas in horizontal rows. Wool thread should not be too thick. Covers the canvas fairly well.

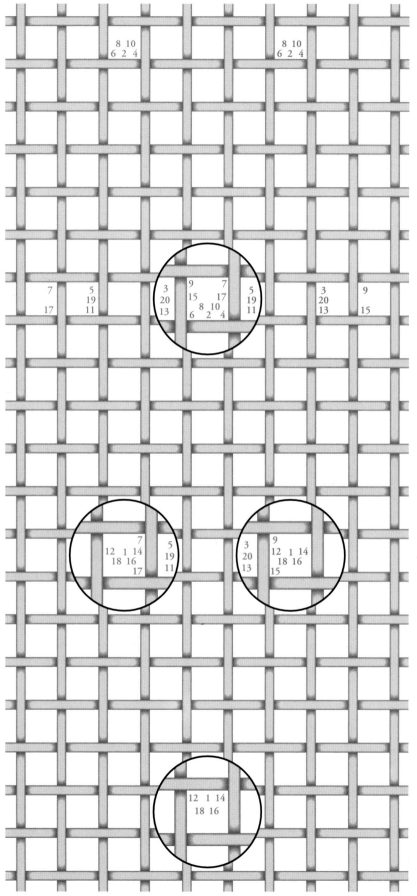

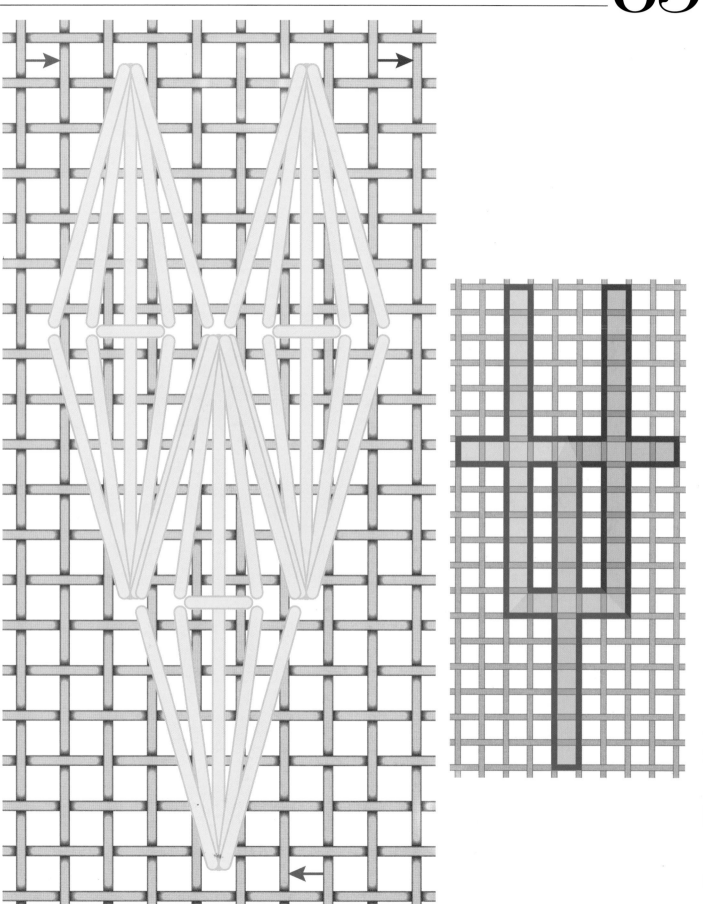

Gate Stitch

86

Stitched on monofil canvas in vertical rows. Medium wool thread thickness. Turn the canvas at the end of each row. Covers canvas fairly well.

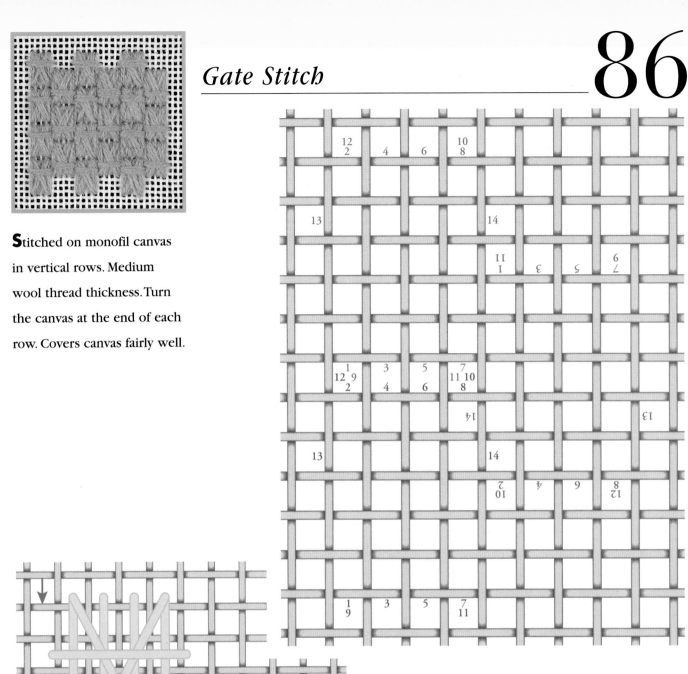

Bourdon Stitch

87

Can be stitched on either monofil or penelope canvas. This stitch is a border and is often used to surround a finished piece of tapestry. For monofil, the wool thread must be very thick.

On the diagram for penelope (left), the numbers for the corner are in red, but you work them at the same time as you do the sides. Stitch 17-18 on both diagrams covers the seam of the corner. You do not have to use this stitch if your seam is faultless or if you just don't want to use it.

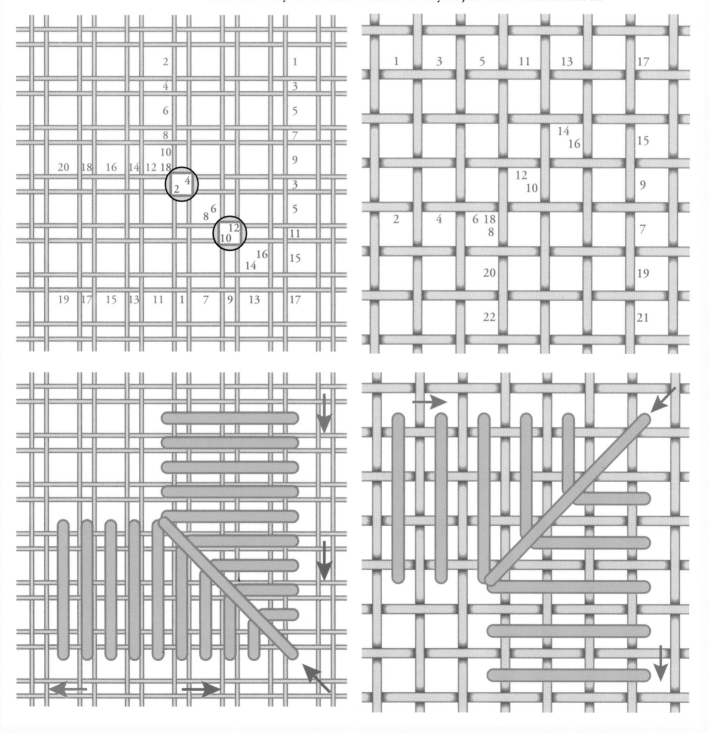

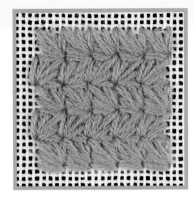

Ray Stitch

Stitched on monofil canvas in horizontal rows. Medium wool thread thickness. Does not entirely cover the canvas.

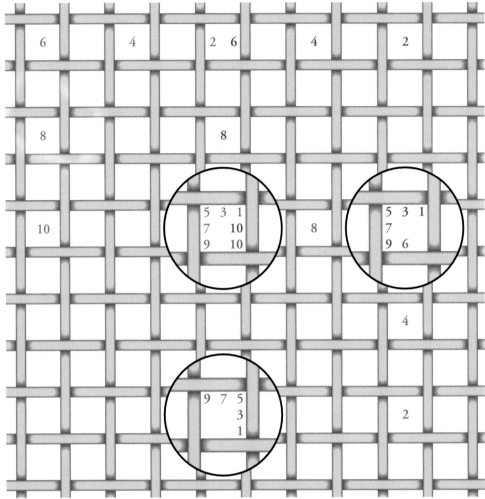

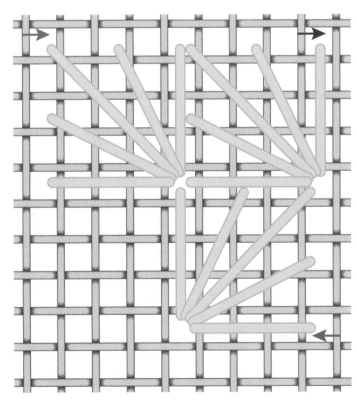

Star Stitch

Stitched on monofil canvas
in horizontal or vertical rows.
Use very thick thread. Does
not cover the canvas well.
It is a good idea to add cross
or simple stitches in the
blank spaces.

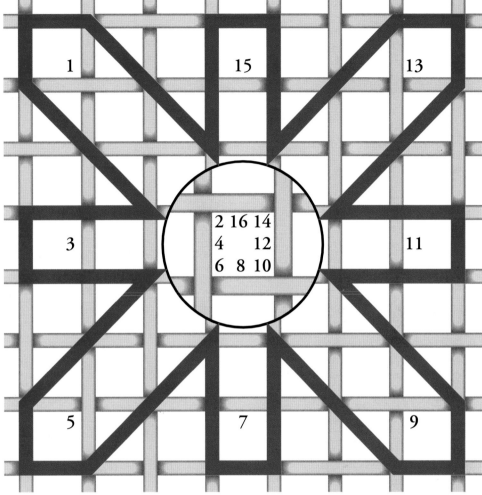

1   15   13

2 16 14
4   12
6 8 10

3   11

5   7   9

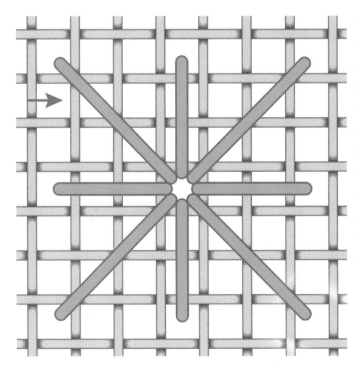

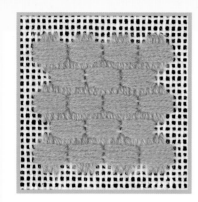

Long Straight Cross Stitch

Worked on monofil canvas in
horizontal rows. Use a thick
thread. Covers the canvas well.

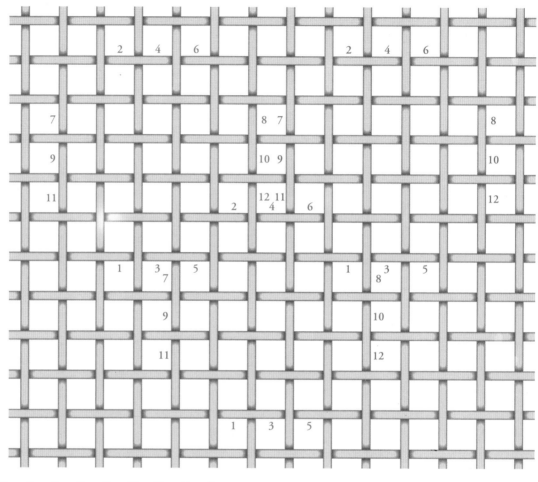

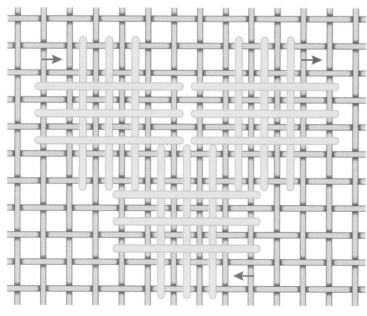

Double Cross Stitch

Stitched on monofil canvas in horizontal rows. Worked in two steps with two colors. Once the crosses are finished, frame them in the other color and add a small cross in the center of four figures. Use a fairly thick wool thread. Covers the canvas well.

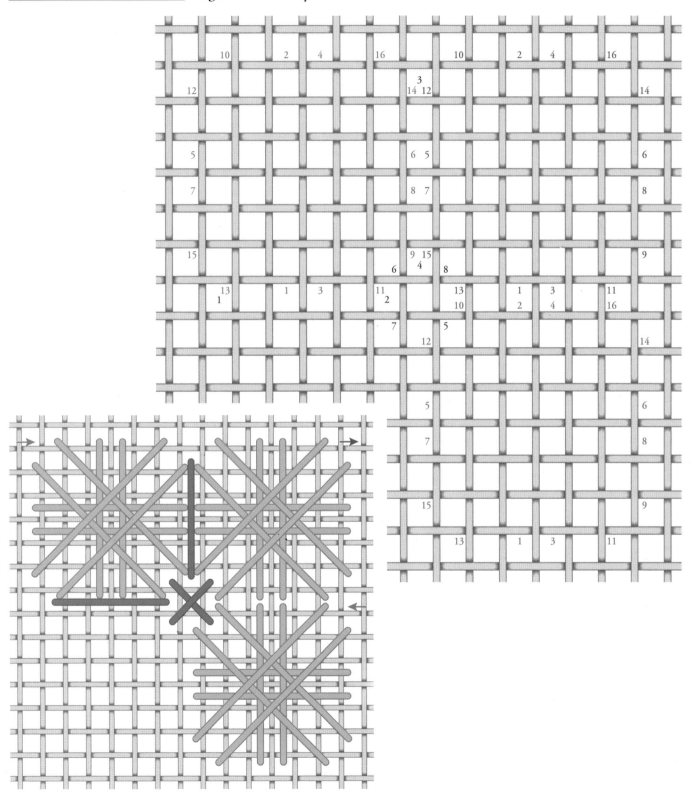

Woven Double Cross

92

Stitched on monofil in horizontal rows. Worked in two steps with two colors, just as in the double cross (p. 119). Use a thick wool thread. Covers the canvas well.

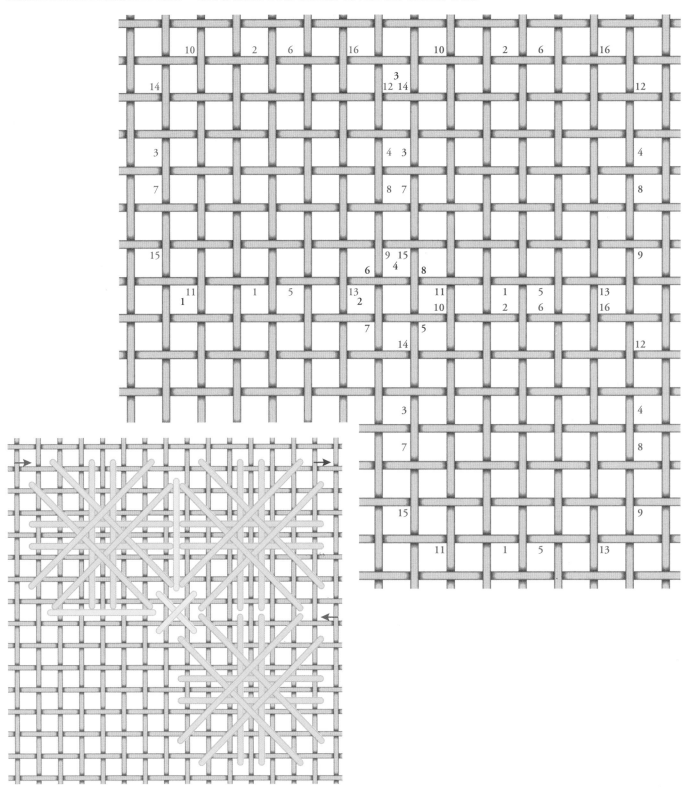

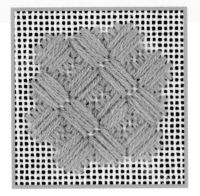

Long Diagonal Cross

Worked on monofil canvas in diagonal rows. Use a thick wool thread. Covers the canvas fairly well.

This is an interesting stitch because each figure is offset by one mesh and contrary to each other. Follow the numbers very carefully.

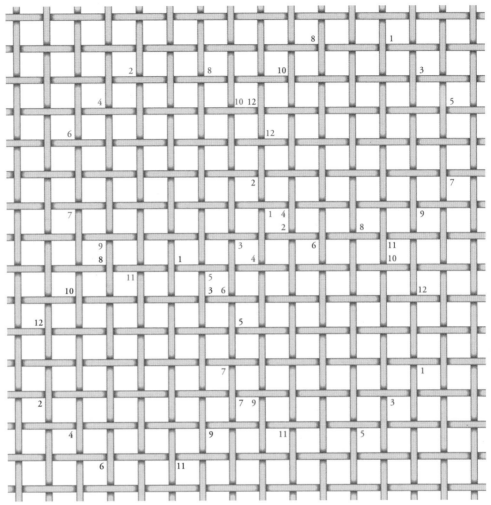

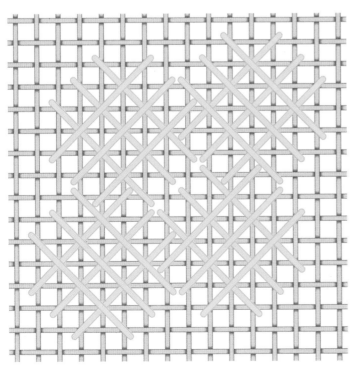

Vaulted Stitch

Stitched on monofil, horizontal or vertical rows. Use thick wool thread. Turn the canvas to stitch each figure. Covers canvas fairly well.

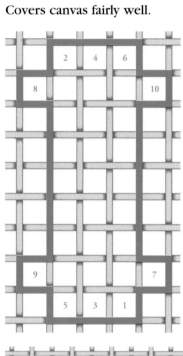

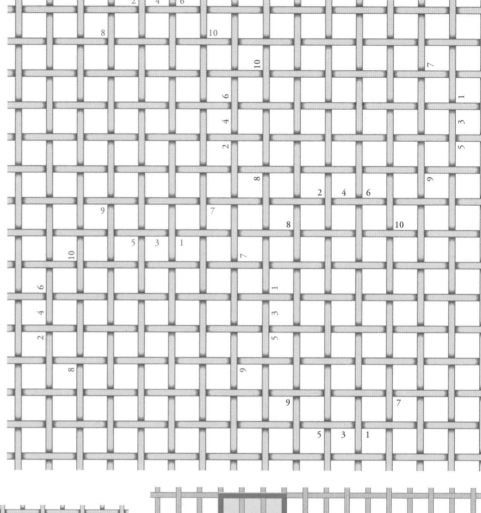

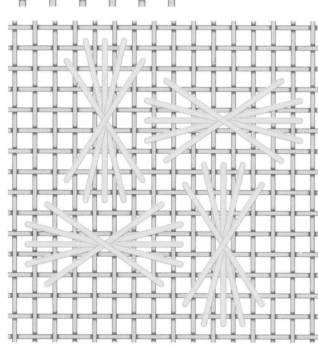

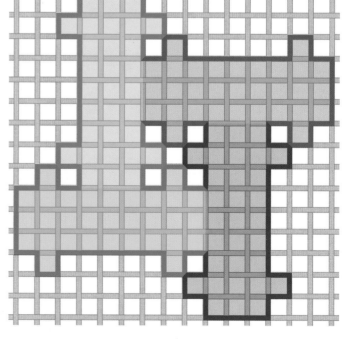

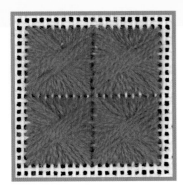

Cabochon (Rhodes Stitch)

Stitched on monofil canvas. Can be used singly or in
horizontal or vertical rows. Medium thick wool. Be sure
the wool is very straight and smooth (not twisted).
Covers the canvas well.

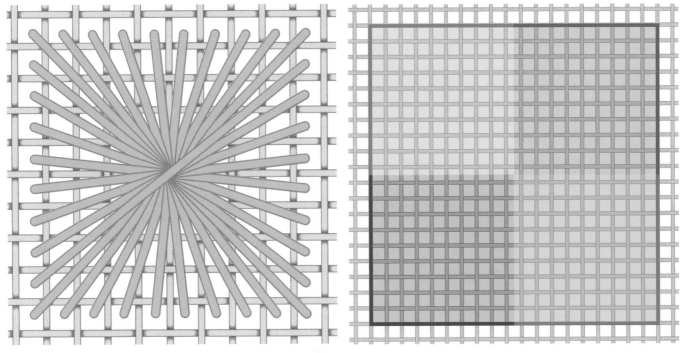

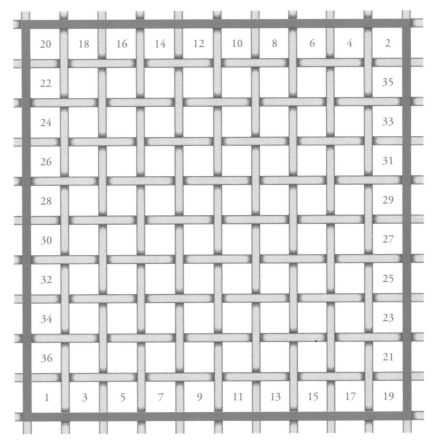

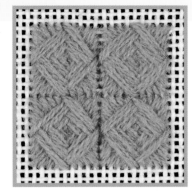

Waffle Stitch

Stitched on monofil canvas. Use a thin wool thread. Can be used as a single figure or worked in horizontal or vertical rows. Covers the canvas well.

Follow the numbers carefully. At #36, pass the needle under #29 before pushing needle into the last hole (indicated by blue arrow on last diagram).

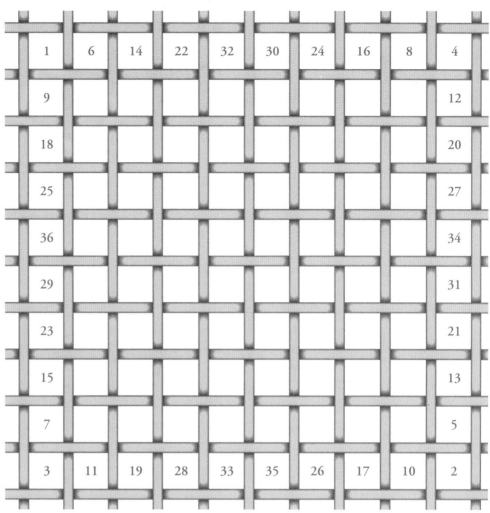

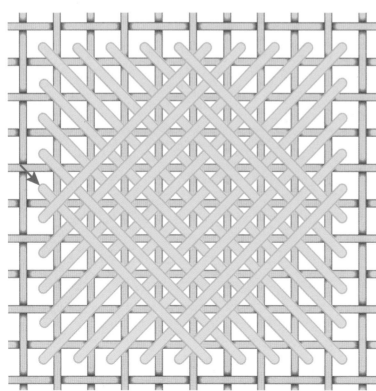

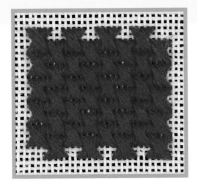

Rhodes Half Stitch

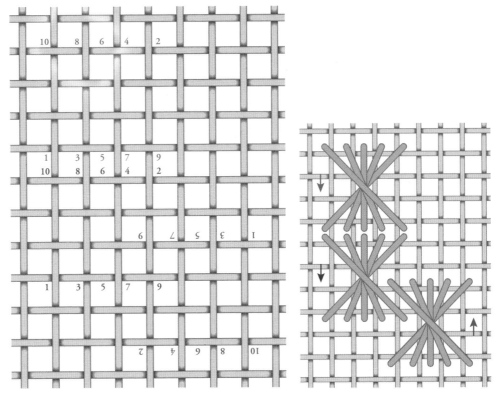

Worked on monofil canvas in vertical rows. At the end of the first row, turn the canvas around and start the second row. You can work this stitch across different mesh counts, but always use an odd number. Use a thick wool thread. Covers canvas very well.

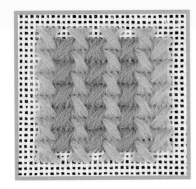

Rhodes Contrary Half Stitch

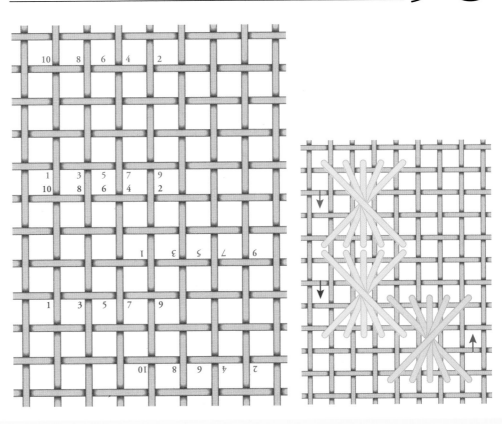

Worked on monofil in vertical rows. This is the Rhodes half stitch, but each row is worked contrarywise. At the end of each row, reverse the canvas so you will stitch always from top to bottom. Use a thick thread. Covers the canvas very well.

Rhodes Octagonal Stitch

Worked on monofil canvas. Use
thick thread. If you stitch several
figures, there should be a square
left in the center of each set of
four figures; stitch a cabochon
(p. 123) to cover the square space.
Covers the canvas very well.

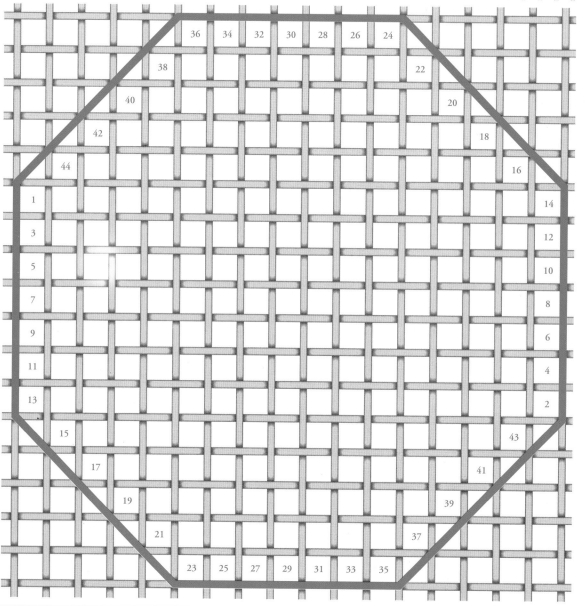

BIBLIOGRAPHY

Coats, J. and P. *50 Points de tapisserie à l'aiguille.* Paris: C. Bernheim Fils. (Out of print.)

Coss, Melinda. *Floral Needlepoint.* London: Anaya Publishers, 1991.

Dyer, Anne, and Valerie Duthoit. *Canvas Work from the Start.* London: G. Bell & Sons, 1972.

Lanz, Sherlee, and Maggie Lane. *A Pageant of Pattern for Needlepoint Canvas.* Andre Deutsch, 1973.

Perrone, Lisbeth. *The New World of Needlepoint.* New York: Random House, 1972.

Phelan, Dorothy. *Florentine Canvaswork.* London: T. Batsford, 1991.

Rhodes, Mary. *Needlepoint: The Art of Canvas Embroidery.* Octopus Books, 1974.

Rogers, Gay Ann. *Tribal Designs for Needlepoint.* Garden City, N.Y.: Doubleday & Co., 1977.

Rome, Carol Cheney. *A New Look at Bargello.* New York: Crown Publishers, 1973.

Thomas, Mary. *L'Encyclopédie de la broderie.* Paris: Fleurus, 1989.